# WOMEN OF OUR TIME

# WOMEN OF OUR TIME

## 75 PORTRAITS OF REMARKABLE WOMEN

FREDERICK S. VOSS
PREFACE BY COKIE ROBERTS

National Portrait Gallery
Smithsonian Institution
Washington, D.C.

**MERRELL**
LONDON · NEW YORK

*Women of Our Time* first published 2002 by Merrell Publishers Limited

This abridged, compact edition first published 2007 by Merrell Publishers Limited

Head office:
81 Southwark Street
London SE1 0HX

New York office:
49 West 24th Street, 8th Floor
New York, NY 10010

merrellpublishers.com

*in association with*

National Portrait Gallery
Smithsonian Institution
8th and F Streets, NW
Washington, D.C.

A catalog record for this book is available from the Library of Congress.

British Library Cataloguing-in-Publication Data:
Voss, Frederick
Women of our time : 75 portraits of remarkable women. –
Compact ed.
1. Women – United States – Biography 2. Portrait photography – United States 3. Women – United States – Pictorial works 4. Celebrities – United States – Biography 5. Celebrities – United States – Pictorial works
I. Title II. National Portrait Gallery (Smithsonian Institution)
305.4′0973′0222

ISBN-13: 978-1-8589-4396-1
ISBN-10: 1-8589-4396-5

Produced by Merrell Publishers Limited
Project coordinator: Dru Dowdy, National Portrait Gallery

Printed and bound in China

Front cover details (left to right, from top): Berenice Abbott, self-portrait, circa 1932 (see p. 62); Margaret Bourke-White, photographer Philippe Halsman, 1943 (see p. 93); Mae West, photographer C. Kenneth Lobben, 1935 (see p. 74); Helen Keller, photographer Charles Whitman, 1904 (see p. 30); Diana Vreeland, photographer Arnold Newman, 1974 (see p. 162); Billie Holiday, photographer Sid Grossman, circa 1948 (see p. 113)

Back cover details (left to right, from top): Gertrude Simmons Bonnin (Zitkala-Ša), photographer Joseph T. Keiley, 1901, from 1898 negative (see p. 29); Lillian Gish, photographer Alfred Cheney Johnston, 1922 (see p. 50); Marian Anderson, photographer Philippe Halsman, 1945 (see p. 102); Katharine Hepburn, photographer Edward Steichen, 1933 (see p. 69); Amelia Earhart, unidentified photographer for International News Photos, 1936 (see p. 78); Sylvia Plath, photographer Rollie McKenna, 1959 (see p. 145)

Page 2: Anne Sexton, photographer Rollie McKenna, 1961 (see p. 149)

Pages 26–27: Dorothy Day, photographer Vivian Cherry, 1955 (see p. 138)

# Contents

# Foreword

This volume is, in part at least, a testament to how far the National Portrait Gallery has come in its photograph collecting in a remarkably short time. The original congressional statute of 1962 that created the Gallery expressly excluded photographic portraits from the museum's collecting mandate. Behind that prohibition was a fear that if the Gallery embarked on collecting photographs, it would place itself in an unseemly competition with yet another federal institution, the Library of Congress. By 1973, however, five years after the Gallery had opened its doors to the public, many individuals concerned with shaping the museum's future were realizing just how unfortunate that collecting restriction was, especially in light of photography's overwhelming importance in the modern portrait tradition. In that year, Gallery commissioner and distinguished art historian Jules Prown wrote to his fellow commissioner Nicholas Brown, "For a museum dedicated to the history of the United States as seen through the lives of its citizens, photographs are documentary material of primary importance through much of the nineteenth and all of the twentieth centuries." Out of that conviction eventually came action. Within another two years, a move was afoot to persuade Congress to permit the Gallery to acquire photographs, and in early 1976, Congress authorized the change. A year later, the museum's Department of Photographs came into existence and began assembling its photographic collection of eminent Americans.

Since then, that collection, starting from almost nothing, has grown at a phenomenal rate. Today it numbers well over ten thousand images and contains works by many of the greatest American portrait photographers—from Mathew Brady and Alexander Gardner, to Alfred Stieglitz, Edward Steichen, and Berenice Abbott, to Arnold Newman, Irving Penn, and Hans Namuth. Thanks to this rapid but discriminating growth under the able direction of the Gallery's photography curators, the Portrait Gallery has been able to assemble this richly varied photographic cross section of noteworthy women of the twentieth century.

For a historian such as myself with a passionate interest in biography, perhaps the most riveting dimension of the photographs selected for this book is the texture of personalities they evoke and the biographical moments they often mark. It is fascinating, for example, to look at Ida Berman's picture of Rosa Parks, which is so suggestive of a mild, rather self-effacing character, and to note that not long after the likeness was made, its subject would spark one of the most salient events of the twentieth century's civil rights movement. Then there is Carl Van Vechten's scowling image of Emma Goldman, taken when she was in her mid-sixties, in which she looks every inch the militant and unrepentant anarchist that she was—still ready to take on the establishment at a moment's notice.

In looking over the portraits of *Women of Our Time*, I also find it an interesting exercise to consider some of them in juxtaposition with one another. One learns, for example, that there are all manner of ways to record for posterity an actress's triumph—from Alfredo Valente's formally posed likeness of Helen Hayes in the title role of *Victoria Regina* to Ruth Orkin's snapshot-like picture of young Julie Harris awkwardly poised to take a sip of coffee following her much-lauded opening-night performance in *The Member of the Wedding*. But as a measure of the great cultural shifts that occurred in the twentieth century, maybe the most telling of the juxtapositions here are the pictures of the nation's first congresswoman, Jeannette Rankin, dating from about 1917, and Texas Congresswoman Barbara Jordan, taken in 1976. Rankin's likeness by L. Chase resonates with a gloved decorum that seems all too anxious to reassure the viewer of her traditional femininity. In an age none too comfortable with women venturing into the political arena, that was entirely understandable. By the mid-1970s, however, such reassurances were not necessary, and Jordan's likeness by Richard Avedon is strictly about forcefulness of personality irrespective of gender.

Many people have been involved in the realization of *Women of Our Time*. Two of the most crucial were Kimberlee Staking and Carla Freudenburg, who provided so much of the research material that served as the basis for the text. We are also enormously indebted to ABC news commentator Cokie Roberts for her wonderful introduction to the book. Finally, there is the Portrait Gallery's former senior historian, Frederick Voss, the book's author. He tells me that he has rarely enjoyed working on a publication as much as he did this one, and this is one reader who thinks it shows.

Marc Pachter
*Director*
*National Portrait Gallery*
*Smithsonian Institution*

# Preface

## Women of Our Time: Firmly on Their Feet
### Cokie Roberts

L
ook into the eyes of the subjects of these photographs and you see the triumphs, failures, hopes, and disappointments of some of the truly talented women of our time. Here you'll find athletes and actresses, scholars and singers, designers and dancers, politicians and playwrights, authors and artists, poets and photographers, evangelists and entrepreneurs, and aviators, architects, and activists of all kinds. All they have in common is their century and their sex, but that's quite a lot in a century when women found themselves in the midst of a revolution. Some fomented it, some floundered through it, and some foundered upon it, but none could ignore the seismic shift in women's lives that the twentieth century produced.

This book gives us the opportunity not only to see the faces of these women, many of them very familiar, but also to "hear" their words and the words of people who knew them or their work. We always knew that Amelia Earhart loved flying, for instance, but when we see a picture of her smiling out from the unfinished fuselage of a Lockheed Electra, she looks as though she's part of the airplane itself, as if she's the engine. For sixteen years after the day in 1921 when she got her first "flying machine," Earhart broke records and made history until she set off for a round-the-world adventure. When she called her husband from India, and he asked if she was having a good time, she shot back, "You betja." It's comforting to know that the woman who disappeared over the South Pacific two weeks later was thoroughly enjoying herself.

Or take the picture of Fannie Lou Hamer, singing and sweating her way through the March Against Fear from Memphis to Jackson in 1966. The forcefulness of the photograph gives a sense of why the term "black power" came into the political vocabulary. Despite the power of the image, however, it's Hamer's words that continue to ring through the decades.

HELEN KELLER 1880–1968
By Charles Whitman
(active 1890s–1900s)
Toned platinum print
22.6 × 16.9 cm ($8^{15}/_{16}$ × $6^{11}/_{16}$ in.)
1904

For many involved in the civil rights movement at the time, her famous saying "I'm sick and tired of being sick and tired" became a rallying cry. This uneducated plantation worker risked her life and livelihood to exercise her right to vote. And then, in organizing other blacks to protest the all-white delegation at the Democratic National Convention of 1964, she helped provide the momentum that culminated in the Voting Rights Act of 1965. That revolutionary legislation so changed the face of American politics that Mississippi went from a state where blacks faced danger if they dared to register to vote to a state with the highest number of African American elected officials in the country.

One of those given the task of memorializing the civil rights movement was Maya Lin, who designed the Civil Rights Memorial in Montgomery, Alabama. She was in the process of conceptualizing that work when the photographer came to her studio and found Lin with her cat. By then she was already famous as the controversial architect behind the Vietnam Memorial in Washington, D.C. Although some in the artistic community and various Vietnam veterans organizations fought against her somber slabs of black stone, her plan was eventually executed, and the Vietnam Memorial is now the most visited site of any in the nation's capital. Millions of people every year run their fingers over the names of the war dead engraved in the stone, silently paying tribute. In defending their choice of Lin's concept, the judges called it "a memorial of our own times." They could not have known how true that would turn out to be.

At a polar extreme from Lin's distracted gaze past her cat is the highly posed picture of one of the great celebrities of the century, Mae West. With her bleached blond ringlets carefully arranged on her head and her white fur draped around her gardenia-bedecked beaded dress, she holds a cigarette in her bejeweled hand as tuxedoed men with lighters at the ready swarm in around her. It was 1935, and she was one of the highest-paid performers in

Hollywood. But again, it's not West's carefully calibrated appearance that lives on; it's her words. "Come up and see me sometime," said in a sultry voice with a come-hither look, has become as familiar a phrase as "To be or not to be." Countless quotation collections throughout the years have offered up some of West's more delightful observations, among them "Too much of a good thing can be wonderful" and "Between two evils I always pick the one I never tried before."

Think of Mae West sharing an exhibit with Helen Keller and Dorothy Day! How different could the outrageous movie star be from the terrified child who was struck deaf and blind or the selfless social worker? Most of us know the remarkable story of Keller's emergence from a dark and soundless world through the efforts of her teacher, Anne Sullivan, and of how she became a spokeswoman for the American Foundation for the Blind. Keller is pictured here smelling a rose and touching braille, using two of her remaining senses. About her work, she wrote, "The field in which I may work is narrow, but it stretches before me limitless. I am like the philosopher whose garden was small but reached up to the stars."

Dorothy Day believed the world was a garden she could nurture to thrive despite inhospitable conditions. As the cofounder of the *Catholic Worker*, Day preached against poverty and war and practiced what she preached through the Catholic Worker Houses of Hospitality, which served as homeless shelters and soup kitchens across the country. Pictured here in her New York newspaper office, Day evinces a toughness that mirrored that of her newspaper. But she was wary of the accolades heaped on her. "When they say you are a saint," she said, "what they mean is that you are not to be taken seriously." How wonderfully wise!

That, in the end, is what binds these women together—their wisdom. Some of their actual words of wisdom have become famous. We've listened over the decades to Julia Child's common sense from the kitchen, even as she creates some impossibly difficult concoction. (It's somehow heartening to know that her husband considered himself a "Cordon Bleu widower." Clearly, we are not dealing with your average cooking enthusiast here.) Equally compelling is the single-minded conviction of "Babe" Didrikson Zaharias, believed by some to have been the greatest female athlete of the century. A spectator marveling at her golf game remarked, "She must be Superman's sister." But Didrikson's explanation was somewhat earthier: "I just loosen my girdle and let the ball have it." Frances Perkins, Franklin Roosevelt's first secretary of labor, had a similar no-nonsense approach. When confronted by an opponent's assertion that her cabinet job was not appropriate for a female, she replied, "The accusation that I am a woman is incontrovertible." End of argument. Then there's Gypsy Rose Lee's insightful observation, "You don't have to be naked to look naked. You just have to think naked." Or Helena Rubinstein's pragmatic conviction, "It doesn't matter how shaky a woman's hand is. She can still apply makeup."

Some of these women show such strength and self-awareness that their pictures and prose make you stand up a little straighter. There's the first woman in Congress, Jeannette Rankin of Montana, elected before national suffrage. She cast one of the few votes against World War I and lost her seat. Decades of activism later, she returned to Congress in the election of 1940, just in time for the bombing of Pearl Harbor. This time hers was the only vote against World War II. Now her words on that occasion, "I cannot vote for war," are etched in marble at the base of a statue of Rankin that is displayed in one of the most prominent corridors of the Capitol.

Gertrude Simmons Bonnin, as the founder of the National Council of American Indians, fought ferociously for the rights of Native Americans. "Sometimes," she once said, "I think I do not even fear God." Designer Pauline Trigère had an equally apt description of herself: She was not good at drawing, she admitted, but "put a piece of fabric in my hands and magic happens." And you can almost hear the strong bass tones of politician Barbara Jordan's voice with her simple statement that she "never wanted to be run of the mill." That understatement is bound to bring a smile.

These fine photographs will coax both smiles and furrowed brows as they bring these remarkable women to life in all their variety. Combined with their subjects' stories, they come close to a shared biography of the women of our time. It's a story that's best summed up by Katharine Graham, the publisher of the *Washington Post*, who unexpectedly took over the newspaper after her husband committed suicide. What she did at that moment, she later recalled, was "shut my eyes and step off the ledge. The surprise was that I landed on my feet." That's been the surprise in many women's lives over the last century as they took on new tasks that were thrust upon them or that they struggled to have the opportunity to tackle. This book presents some of the best of those women, firmly on their feet.

# Introduction

The time frame for this book is the twentieth century, a hundred-year span that was remarkable for a host of landmark changes in the way we conduct our lives and what we expect from the world at large—from the advent of the airplane and the car to incredible leaps in medicine's ability to save lives, the miracle of space travel, and the emergence of a workplace-transforming computer technology. Many of the figures featured in *Women of Our Time* both reflected and enacted one of America's most important twentieth-century stories—the shifting role of women and their ever-enlarging significance in all branches of endeavor.

When the twentieth century began, most American women did not have the right to vote, much less hold public office, and the chances of winning the franchise any time soon seemed quite remote. In 1901, the expectations for most women were limited in a host of other ways as well. To marry a good provider and look after his household and children was just about all most conventional middle-class women dared hope for. Although a college education had been an option for American women for some time, precious few of them went beyond high school. And if a woman had to work outside the home or simply chose to do so, the options, generally speaking, were on the sparse and none-too-lucrative side. Maids were always in demand, of course, and it was possible to get various types of factory work deemed suitable for a woman. For the better-educated woman, a career in teaching was an option. But heaven help the woman who

FRANCES PERKINS 1880–1965
By Clara E. Sipprell (1885–1975)
Gelatin silver print
25.2 × 20.3 cm (9 ¹⁵/₁₆ × 8 in.)
1952

might aspire to becoming a doctor, a lawyer, an engineer, a journalist, or a business executive. Although it was not altogether impossible to achieve such career goals, any woman setting her sights on them in 1900 would have to understand that the profession she had chosen was difficult to attain at best and, if she was not endowed with an uncommon supply of fortitude, probably impossible.

By the close of the twentieth century, however, so much of that had changed. Not only could women vote, but no one was batting an eye when one of them won election to an alderman's seat, a state governorship, or the United States Senate. With two women sitting on the Supreme Court, a woman occupant in the Oval Office seemed only a matter of time. As for education and career options, while American women perhaps still had grounds for complaint of being held back in some areas, the choices were, by and large, as expansive as they were for males. From the armed forces and space exploration to corporate management, stock brokering, and law enforcement, the presence of a woman had largely ceased to be a novelty worthy of notice.

It is fair to say that virtually all the individuals included in this book were in one degree or another affected by this transformation as it played itself out around them. Doubtless the opportunities for their distinctions were shaped in part by the twentieth century's increasingly open-ended environment for feminine achievement. But maybe a more significant point to be made is that so many of these women were themselves significant instruments in creating and fostering that environment. On the political front, there are, for example, Jeannette Rankin, whose election to the House of Representatives in 1916 marked the beginning of a female presence in Congress, and Secretary of Labor Frances Perkins, whose long tenure in Franklin Roosevelt's cabinet accustomed the nation to seeing a woman as a high-level presidential adviser. In the realm of ideas and activism that had direct impact in enlarging the definition of women's potential, there are birth-control advocate Margaret Sanger, who helped transform child-bearing from being a woman's inevitable lot to a matter of personal choice; journalist-editor Gloria Steinem, who ranked among the leading figures in the feminist movement of the late 1960s and 1970s; and anthropologist Margaret Mead, some of whose research yielded evidence that the roles of males and females—once widely believed to be biologically preordained—might in large part be the result of environmental conditioning [fig. 1]. And in the world of corporate enterprise, there are cosmetics entrepreneur Helena Rubinstein, whose skill in driving a bargain clearly gave lie to the notion that women had no head for business, and Katharine Graham, who surprised even herself with her stellar success as the first female chief executive officer of a Fortune 500 company.

This book, however, is as much about the art of photographic portraiture as it is about female achievements. Among the images featured in it are works by such distinguished photographers of the twentieth century as Adolph de Meyer, Edward Steichen, Louise Dahl-Wolfe [fig. 2], Philippe Halsman, Irving Penn,

1  Lotte Jacobi's self-portrait has a staged quality that stands in sharp
contrast to the understated naturalism of her likeness of anthropologist
Margaret Mead.

Lotte Jacobi (1896–1990), self-portrait, gelatin silver print, 1936
(circa 1950 print). National Portrait Gallery, Smithsonian Institution

Lotte Jacobi, Arnold Newman, and Lisette Model [fig. 3]. But perhaps more noteworthy is the diversity in approach to portraiture that is to be found in this selection of likenesses. Thus, while the images of Native American reformer Gertrude Simmons Bonnin by Joseph T. Keiley and dancer Isadora Duncan by Arnold Genthe epitomize the soft-focus pictorialism that held wide sway early in the century, a number of likenesses—including Ruth Orkin's shot of actress Julie Harris negotiating an awkward sip of coffee at an opening-night party—belong to a journalistic brand of portraiture that places a high premium on in-situ candor. Yet other pictures owe their inspiration to an unapologetically theatrical style of photography—Steichen's Katharine Hepburn [fig. 4] and Nickolas Muray's Anna May Wong, for example—that reached its most obvious flowering in the Hollywood publicity glamour still. In sharp contrast to that artificiality is the unadorned, almost naive simplicity of Ida Berman's photograph of civil rights activist Rosa Parks and the indifferent casualness of Fred Stein's likeness of political thinker and historian Hannah Arendt.

In one degree or another, photographic portraits are biographical documents. As such, they perform their most basic function by telling us what a person looks like. But often they go beyond mere physical inventory to enlarge or reinforce our more qualitative understandings about the individual we are confronting. A prime case in point to be found in these pages is Adolph de Meyer's photograph of silent-screen actress Mary Pickford, which so fully

2  The maker of Katharine Cornell's likeness, fashion photographer
Louise Dahl-Wolfe, contemplates one of her pictures in a *Harper's
Bazaar* cover layout.

Hans L. Jorgensen (born 1915), gelatin silver print, 1941.
National Portrait Gallery, Smithsonian Institution

captures the sense of innocent vulnerability that was for so much of her career the main source of her box-office appeal [fig. 5]. Yet two other good examples are Arnold Newman's likeness of cosmetics entrepreneur Helena Rubinstein [fig. 6], which evokes so persuasively her hard-driving and at times tempestuous nature, and Vivian Cherry's picture of Dorothy Day, which speaks volumes about the stoic dedication of this intensely religious Catholic reformer. Finally, there is Linda McCartney's picture of singer Janis Joplin in performance, taken just as she was emerging as a major pop music star. Looking at Joplin's intensely contorted image, one can almost feel firsthand the impact on audiences of her shrill, high-voltage, rasping style.

Among the most biographically compelling of the likenesses in *Women of Our Time*, for this writer at least, are those that belong to an especially significant moment in the subject's career. The image of Amelia Earhart by an unidentified photographer, for example, amply records the clean-scrubbed, tomboyish allure that so enhanced her celebrity as America's most celebrated female aviator. More significant, however, it records Earhart serenely looking out from the nose of the yet-to-be-completed plane that was being made for her flight around the

3 Photographer Lisette Model's interest in jazz and modern dance led her to make likenesses of singer Ella Fitzgerald and dancer Pearl Primus.

Todd Webb (1905–2000), gelatin silver print, 1948. National Portrait Gallery, Smithsonian Institution

4 Edward Steichen's likeness of himself bespeaks his abiding interest
in creating pattern in his portrait photography, which is also evident in
his picture of Olympic swimmers Eleanor Holm and Helene Madison.

Edward Steichen (1879–1973), self-portrait, gelatin silver print, 1929.
National Portrait Gallery, Smithsonian Institution; acquired in memory
of Agnes and Eugene Meyer through the generosity of Katharine
Graham and the New York Community Trust, The Island Fund

world, a venture that was destined to end tragically with her death somewhere in the South Pacific. Then there is Harry Warnecke's smiling photograph of the Hollywood child star Shirley Temple. Temple was ten in the picture and enjoying an incredible popularity. But the image does not stop at depicting the dimpled charm undergirding that popularity; it also hints at an incipient maturity that would increasingly erode Temple's effectiveness in the precocious little-girl roles that had made her famous.

Yet another image imbued with more than the usual biographical salience is the picture snapped by Navy medic David Geary in the winter of 1954. The subject is Marilyn Monroe as she entertained American soldiers in Korea, and perhaps it should be titled *Marilyn's Epiphany*. Filled with fears and insecurities she would never entirely overcome, Monroe was amazed at the overwhelming enthusiasm her performances generated, and it was that enthusiasm, she later said, that convinced her at last of what had been clear to others for some time—that she was truly a star of the first magnitude. And finally, there is Bob Willoughby's picture of Judy Garland on the set of *A Star Is Born*. The picture is a memento of one of Garland's finest

5  Adolph de Meyer created the soft-focus image of silent-screen star Mary Pickford.

Adolph de Meyer (1868–1946), self-portrait, gelatin silver print, circa 1920. National Portrait Gallery, Smithsonian Institution

6  Arnold Newman typically shot his likenesses of such
personalities as strip artist Gypsy Rose Lee and cosmetics
entrepreneur Helena Rubinstein against backgrounds evocative
of their character and occupations.

Arnold Newman (1918–2006), self-portrait, gelatin silver
print, 1987. National Portrait Gallery, Smithsonian Institution;
gift of Arnold Newman

film performances in the making, but there is a dark, brooding edge to it that bespeaks the personal turmoil that plagued this gifted woman's career to the end and made even many of her triumphs a source of unhappiness.

In closing, something should perhaps be said about the selection of the individuals picked for this book. Readers might wonder why some women of obvious importance are not included here. In large degree, the answer lies in the fact that the National Portrait Gallery's photography collection was established only in 1976. Since then, the collection has had impressive growth and now contains many substantial treasures in American portrait photography, including a good many of the images reproduced here. But in terms of building a comprehensive collection, a quarter century is not a long time. We can only hope that in the coming years the museum's photographic holdings will become richer yet, and that future acquisitions will encompass a plenitude of likenesses that will further enrich the Gallery's capacity to tell the story of women in the twentieth century—and, for that matter, the twenty-first as well.

WOMEN OF OUR TIME

The daughter of a Sioux mother and a white father, Gertrude Simmons Bonnin spent her early childhood on the Yankton Reservation in what is now South Dakota. At age eight, she left the reservation to embark on an education that included attending a Quaker-run school in Indiana and two years of study at Earlham College. While taking advantage of these educational opportunities, Bonnin was nevertheless troubled that they were distancing her from her Native American culture. That thought festered even more when Bonnin began teaching at Carlisle Indian School in Pennsylvania, where assimilation into white society was a primary goal. Likening her situation there to that of an uprooted tree, she later wrote, "I was shorn of my branches. . . . The natural coat of bark which had protected my oversensitive nature was scraped off to the very quick."

Among Bonnin's efforts to deal with this sense of rootlessness was the compilation of Native American lore that she had heard as child, entitled *Old Indian Legends,* and published in 1901 under her Native American name, Zitkala-Ša. Bonnin, however, found the ultimate resolution of her identity crisis in activism dedicated to advancing Native American rights. In 1916, she became secretary of the Society of American Indians, and soon emerged as one of its most valuable spokespersons. In 1926, she founded the National Council of American Indians, which became one of the most effective forces in redressing the injustices of the government's Indian policies. Of her readiness to challenge the federal establishment, she once said, "sometimes I think I do not even fear God."

This image was made in 1898, while Bonnin was teaching at Carlisle. The photographer was Joseph T. Keiley, a member of the Photo Secession movement, which promoted recognition of photography as an art form.

# Gertrude Simmons Bonnin (Zitkala-Ša)
1876–1938
*Native American reformer, writer*

JOSEPH T. KEILEY
(1869–1914)
Photogravure
15.9 × 9.5 cm (6¼ × 3¾ in.)
1901, from 1898 negative

Helen Keller was born a normal, healthy child. But an illness that struck her at nineteen months left her deaf and blind, and her parents found themselves unable to cope with her needs. As a result, their strong-willed daughter was left essentially to her own devices, and by age five, she had grown into a wildly obstreperous child living in her own world. That situation changed dramatically in March 1887, when Anne Sullivan arrived at Keller's home in Tuscumbia, Alabama, to become her governess. Once blind herself, Sullivan soon penetrated Keller's soundless, dark world, and within a few months Keller was finally connecting to the people around her.

Under Sullivan's tutelage, Keller took on ever-greater learning challenges. In 1900, she entered Radcliffe College and graduated four years later cum laude. In the meantime, she had also written a bestselling autobiography and become a widely revered symbol of the human spirit's indomitability.

In 1924, Keller became an official spokesperson for the newly formed American Foundation for the Blind and quickly proved to be one of its greatest assets. Among her most concrete triumphs was her successful lobbying in the 1930s for a congressional act to fund reading services for the blind.

"Our worst foes are not belligerent circumstances," Keller observed in *The Story of My Life*, "but wavering spirits. . . . The field in which I may work is narrow, but it stretches before me limitless. I am like the philosopher whose garden was small but reached up to the stars."

This image of Keller appeared as the frontispiece for her article in *Century* magazine in January 1905, entitled "A Chat about the Hand." "Paradise," she declared in the first paragraph, "is attained by touch; for in touch is all love and intelligence."

# Helen Keller

1880–1968

*Humanitarian*

CHARLES WHITMAN
(active 1890s–1900s)
Toned platinum print
22.6 × 16.9 cm (8¹⁵⁄₁₆ × 6¹¹⁄₁₆ in.)
1904

Contrary to the prevailing expectations for women in late-nineteenth-century America, Frances Benjamin Johnston did not particularly want the life of a wife and mother. Instead, she wanted to become a painter, and in 1884 she went to Paris to study at the Académie Julian. Over the next few years, the focus of her professional ambitions shifted from studio art to illustration journalism. But then she discovered the potential of the camera, and following periods of training with several photographers, she set out to become America's first woman photojournalist.

Johnston published her first photographs—pictures of the United States Mint—in *Demorest's Family Magazine* in late 1889, and in the early 1890s she turned her camera on life in the Pennsylvania coal regions. The result was an impressive series of pictures that firmly established Johnston as a capable photojournalist. Among her most widely admired works were her photographs of student life at Hampton Institute, a Virginia school for African Americans. Those images—along with her photographs of public education in Washington, D.C.—earned her a gold medal at the Paris Exposition of 1900. In portraiture she counted among her subjects Susan B. Anthony, Mark Twain, Andrew Carnegie, and Booker T. Washington, and the most lasting achievements of her later years were her pictures of the early American architecture of nine southern states.

The evidence is persuasive that this likeness of Johnston was taken in Venice in the summer of 1905, and was probably the work of her traveling companion, portrait photographer Gertrude Käsebier. The two women enjoyed their stay in Venice immensely, owing in part to a third photographer, Baron Adolph de Meyer, who gave them free use of the darkroom in his home on the Grand Canal.

# Frances Benjamin Johnston
1864–1952
*Photographer*

Attributed to
GERTRUDE KÄSEBIER
(1852–1934)
Platinum print
22.2 × 15.7 cm (8¾ × 6³⁄₁₆ in.)
1905

Isadora Duncan grew up in a directionless, bohemian atmosphere that would have left many a youngster feeling lost. She thrived on it, however. By age ten, Duncan knew that she wanted to be a dancer and had already begun to evolve a definition of dance that rejected the rules of classical ballet to embrace improvisation and self-expression.

In her late teens, Duncan began her performing career as a dancer-actress in a New York theatrical company. But she ultimately did not like the work, and after leaving the company, she started giving solo performances premised on her own expressionistic concept of dance. Appreciation for her innovations was scant in America. Europe, however, was another story. Warmly received from Paris to Budapest, Duncan created perhaps her greatest sensation in Berlin, where, following her performances, wildly enthusiastic students drew her carriage through the streets to her hotel. On her return to the United States in 1908, audiences were still somewhat hesitant to accept her. Nevertheless, her circle of admirers was growing. "More like a spirit than a woman," a Philadelphia critic declared, Isadora Duncan was "an embodiment of joy, the lightsome wraith of the veritable spirit of the melody."

Duncan's several efforts at teaching had at best a negligible influence on younger performers. The same cannot be said of her performances, which ultimately exercised an impact that easily places her among the primary founders of modern dance.

Arnold Genthe's picture of Duncan shows her in the classically inspired draped tunic that she often wore on stage. Both a friend and an admirer of Duncan, Genthe noted in his memoirs that she did not have a beautiful body, but "when she danced the nobility of her gestures could make it into something of superb perfection and divine loveliness."

# Isadora Duncan
1877–1927
*Dancer*

ARNOLD GENTHE
(1869–1942)
Gelatin silver print
27.2 × 35.3 cm ($10^{11}/_{16}$ × $13^{7}/_{8}$ in.)
circa 1916

Encouraged as a child to set high goals for herself, Jeannette Rankin rose rapidly in the women's suffrage movement after joining its ranks in 1910. By 1913, she was a field secretary for the National American Woman Suffrage Association, and a year later she orchestrated the successful campaign to enfranchise women in her native Montana.

Rankin now set her sights on running for Congress. Many, including most fellow suffragists, told her she was foolish. Rankin forged ahead anyway, and in November 1916 she became the first woman elected to the U.S. House of Representatives.

Rankin's victory made her into an overnight celebrity. *Literary Digest* proclaimed her "The Girl of the Golden West," and a car business sought to use her in its advertising. But most of all, she was the darling of the suffrage movement. When Rankin arrived in Washington to take her seat in Congress in early 1917, one suffrage leader declared, "Now that we have a pull in Congress, there is no telling what we will accomplish."

Unfortunately, Rankin's rising star was about to plummet. On April 2, President Woodrow Wilson asked Congress to endorse America's entry into World War I. Rankin's political survival, most of her advisers believed, depended on her overcoming her pacifist principles to vote for war. Doing otherwise, they said, risked being dismissed as the stereotypical female sentimentalist. Rankin knew they were right. Nevertheless, when the war vote came up, she voted no.

In doing so, Rankin lost her political credibility and any near-term chances of reelection. The congressional career of this unrelenting pacifist, however, was not entirely over. In 1940, she again claimed a congressional seat, and was present in the House in December 1941 to cast the single negative vote against America's entry into World War II following the Japanese attack on Pearl Harbor.

---

# Jeannette Rankin
1880–1973
*Social activist*

L. CHASE
(active 1910s)
Gelatin silver print
17.2 × 11 cm (6¾ × 4⅜ in.)
circa 1917
Gift of Margaret Sterling Brooke

argaret Sanger had her first taste of reforming activism in 1912, when she began participating in worker strikes. As a maternity nurse working in New York City's Lower East Side, however, she discovered a cause in far greater need of her attention. On her rounds, she kept encountering women whose health had been devastated by excessive child-bearing, and by 1914, she was publishing a feminist magazine called *The Woman Rebel*, a chief focus of which was the advocacy of birth control.

Published in an age that deemed discussion of such matters indecent, the journal was soon shut down. By year's end, Sanger had fled to Europe to avoid trial on charges of disseminating obscenities in the mail. In 1916, however, she was back in the United States, founding a birth-control clinic in Brooklyn. But once again the law frowned on her enterprise. Soon after authorities closed the clinic, Sanger was sentenced to thirty days in prison.

Even so, Sanger's preachings were gradually winning respectability. By 1923, she was able to open in New York City a clinic offering contraceptive advice, without any fear of being closed down. As support for her cause broadened over the next fifteen years, some three hundred birth-control clinics were established across the country.

Taken shortly after Sanger's thirty-day imprisonment, this image evokes one of her greatest assets as leader of a controversial cause: a benignly feminine exterior that often won her sympathetic hearings in quarters where a more militant bearing might not have done. Still, Sanger could be fiercely combative. A case in point was her refusal to let the police take her fingerprints just before her prison release. She emerged from the physical struggle that ensued "bruised and exhausted" but nevertheless triumphant.

# Margaret Sanger
## 1879–1966
### *Reformer*

IRA HILL
(died 1939)
Gelatin silver print
24 × 18.8 cm (9⁷⁄₁₆ × 7⁷⁄₈ in.), 1917
Gift of Margaret Sanger Lampe and Nancy Sanger
Pallesen, granddaughters of Margaret Sanger

Louise Bryant is one of those historical figures remembered less for what they did than for the people with whom they are identified. Possessing an uncommon beauty, she formed her most noteworthy association in the summer of 1914, when the socialist radical journalist John Reed came to Portland, Oregon, to visit his family. Although Bryant seemed happily married to a local dentist, she fell in love with Reed almost immediately, and in December 1915, she left Portland to join him in New York City's bohemian Greenwich Village.

In New York, Bryant worked sporadically as a journalist, and in August 1917, she and Reed set out to cover the Russian Revolution. Arriving in Russia in time to witness the triumph of the Marxian Bolsheviks, Reed and Bryant were hardly unbiased observers. While Reed declared the Bolshevik regime "a kingdom more bright than any heaven had to offer," Bryant was especially entranced with Bolshevism's promise of equality for women.

Personal bias, however, did not prevent Bryant and Reed from doing some good reporting. Of the early accounts of the Bolshevik takeover, none was more widely admired than Reed's *Ten Days That Shook the World.* But Bryant also made a significant contribution to the revolution's early bibliography with her *Six Red Months in Russia.* The book had a human texture that proved a fine complement to the broader picture found in Reed's *Ten Days.* As one reviewer put it, Bryant made readers see the revolution through "the eyes of the people themselves."

It is thought that this photograph dates from late 1918, about the time that *Six Red Months* was published. Bryant was much in demand on the American lecture circuit, despite the country's antipathy for anyone sympathetic to the Bolshevik cause. Two years later, her life with Reed ended after Reed's death from typhus in the Soviet Union.

# Louise Bryant
1885–1936
*Journalist*

ALFRED COHN
(1897–1972)
Gelatin silver print
16.8 × 10.2 cm (6⅝ × 4 in.)
circa 1918

In her youth, Katherine Stinson wanted to be a piano teacher. When she learned that pilots earned up to a thousand dollars a day demonstrating the new miracle of airplane flight, she decided to finance her music education by becoming one of those well-paid pilots. To pay for the flying lessons, she sold her piano, but in the end that did not matter. By the time she received an international pilot's license in July 1912, aviation was her all-consuming passion. Known as the "Flying Schoolgirl," the petite Stinson was soon a regular on the flight exhibition circuit.

Some said that Stinson was the first woman pilot to "loop the loop." More noteworthy, however, was the variant on that feat that she invented in 1915, called the "dippy twist loop," which required rolling her plane wing over wing at the top of each loop. In late 1916, Stinson toured Asia, where her gender made her air exploits all the more fascinating. "The women were wild with excitement," she reported from Japan, "and the men were not far behind."

On returning to the United States, Stinson set new benchmarks for time and distance, with a nonstop flight of 610 miles (982 km) made in just over nine hours. Unfortunately, by 1920 her flying days had ended, owing to tuberculosis. Although she recovered from the illness, she never piloted a plane again.

In her zest for flying, Stinson departed from the feminine norms of her day, but some might have seen in the meticulous care she took in cleaning and maintaining her planes a stereotypical female instinct for tidiness. In truth, that concern had more to do with survival instincts. As she put it, "If your airplane breaks down, you can't sit on a convenient cloud and tinker with [it]."

# Katherine Stinson
## 1891–1977
### *Aviator*

By an unidentified photographer
Gelatin silver print
24.7 × 17.1 cm (9¹¹⁄₁₆ × 6¾ in.)
circa 1919

In 1909, the young actress Mary Pickford had just finished a run on Broadway in *The Warrens of Virginia*, and her prospects for landing a role in a new play seemed poor, in spite of her experience. In desperation, she did what few self-respecting stage actresses cared to do in those days: She applied for a job at moviemaker D.W. Griffith's Biograph Studios. The never-too-tactful Griffith took a look at Pickford and said, "You're too little and too fat." But he hired her anyway, at ten dollars a day. So began the ascent of the silent-film industry's first major star.

Demonstrating a magnetic screen presence from the outset, Pickford proved capable at playing a variety of types. Still, it was her many portrayals of the frail but spunky young innocent that most endeared her to audiences and transformed her into "America's Sweetheart." And with that persona came considerable fortune. By 1916, Pickford was earning ten thousand dollars a week. But as generous as that was, it was probably not enough. The mere fact that Pickford "appears in [a movie]," declared one observer, "makes it a good picture."

Along with being the early film industry's greatest female star, Pickford was almost certainly its most astute businesswoman. By 1918, she had established her own movie company, which increased her earnings on her films substantially. A year later, with Charlie Chaplin, D.W. Griffith, and her soon-to-be husband, Douglas Fairbanks, she became a cofounder of United Artists, a film distribution enterprise that yielded yet greater profits.

This picture dates from Pickford's marriage to fellow screen star Fairbanks, and shows her in her wedding dress. When it appeared in *Vogue*'s February 1920 issue, it ran with a caption observing that "helplessly feminine" as Pickford may look, "she makes every year a tremendous fortune."

# Mary Pickford
1893–1979
*Actress*

ADOLPH DE MEYER
(1868–1946)
Gelatin silver print
23.2 × 18.2 cm (9⅛ × 7⁷⁄₁₆ in.)
1920

At Aimee Semple McPherson's birth in 1890, her mother was determined that her newborn daughter should dedicate herself to the work of God. But in committing young Aimee to that course, she certainly had no inkling of just what that would mean. By her mid-twenties, armed with the flair of a natural performer, McPherson was fast building a reputation as an amazingly stirring evangelical preacher. Between 1918 and 1923, she crisscrossed the United States eight times, often preaching several times a day. But more noteworthy than her rigorous schedule was her crowd-drawing power. During two stays in Denver, she preached to some twelve thousand people every night for a month, and in San Diego she attracted crowds that filled Balboa Park from one end to the other.

Critics sneered at McPherson's histrionics and faith healing. They called her the "whoopee evangelist" and the "Barnum of religion." But even cynics acknowledged her power. Once launched into a performance, admitted one naysayer, she "electrifies every person in the hall."

Evidence suggests that this photograph was taken in the spring of 1921, as McPherson's career was approaching its height. Construction had begun in Los Angeles on the future seat of her Church of the Foursquare Gospel, and within a few years, she would be presiding over a Bible college and radio station. This image was taken in St. Louis, where the initial response to her preaching had been tepid. Then a local newspaper carried a report on her doings, under the headline "MAN BARKS AS WOMEN AND GIRLS … SHRIEK AT REVIVAL." With that, the police had all they could do to prevent people from trampling each other in their attempts to hear McPherson, and thousands had to be turned away from some of her sessions.

# Aimee Semple McPherson

1890–1944

*Evangelist*

GERHARD SISTERS STUDIO
(active 1903–after 1924)
Gelatin silver print
19.5 × 14.2 cm (7¹¹/₁₆ × 5⅝ in.)
circa 1921

T he short, heavyset Gertrude Stein possessed a presence that made her seem destined for the role of a gurulike arbiter, and to a large degree, she lived up to that expectation. In late 1903, assured of ample income from a family inheritance, she settled in Paris with her brother Leo. There, following Leo's lead, she became an avid collector of art by such modernists as Henri Matisse and Pablo Picasso, and as her collection grew, it became the backdrop for salons hosted by Stein. Attended by some of the early twentieth century's most significant avant-garde painters and writers, the gatherings were a social crossroad of modernism, with Stein seated squarely in the center.

But Stein was not just a patron of modernism; she was also one of its more arcane practitioners. Aspiring to a style that was the equivalent of Cubist painting, she produced prose that struck most readers as "soporific rigamaroles." Still, Stein had her admirers. Among them was Ernest Hemingway, whose own work bore traces of her mentoring. Moreover, her engaging memoir, *The Autobiography of Alice B. Toklas*, published in 1933, proved that she could write for the general public and do it with considerable wit.

In the photograph here, Stein poses for her terra-cotta portrait by Jo Davidson. The picture ran with an article on Stein in *Vanity Fair* in February 1923. Also featured was her verbal portrait of sculptor Davidson, which ran in part: "Wives are a great recognition. / There were more husbands than wives in their lives. / Two live too him. / This is the story of Jo Davidson." Davidson recalled that it made sense when Stein herself read it to him, but when he read it later, it was only gibberish.

## Gertrude Stein
## 1874–1946
## with Jo Davidson
*Writer, art collector*

MAN RAY
(1890–1976)
Gelatin silver print
16.9 × 11.8 cm (6⅝ × 4⅝ in.)
circa 1922

In many ways, the silent-screen career of actress Lillian Gish ran parallel to that of her friend Mary Pickford. Both had begun acting at an early age and had traveled many of the same theater circuits. Both also got their start in the silent-film industry working with director D.W. Griffith, and found themselves, especially in their early films, typecast as the innocent, wide-eyed heroine. Gish "played so many frail, downtrodden little virgins," she once recalled, that she began to think she had invented the type.

Despite the parallels, Gish never came close to rivaling Pickford as a box-office draw. In terms of talent, however, Gish may well deserve pride of place as the silent-screen era's finest actress. Her sustained expression of terror in a scene from *Broken Blossoms* in 1919 is still regarded today as one of the greatest acting moments in all of silent film. Equally impressive was Gish's portrayal of Hester Prynne in *The Scarlet Letter* in 1926. "She is not Hawthorne's Hester Prynne," one critic declared, "but she is yours and mine."

No treatment, however brief, of Gish's silent-screen career could fail to mention her performance in D.W. Griffith's *Birth of a Nation,* the movie industry's first feature-length film, released in 1915. Gish was not Griffith's first choice for the major role of Elsie Stoneman, but he thought she would at least be adequate in the part. Gish's performance exceeded that expectation by a good deal and proved a significant factor in the film's success.

Gish is dressed in this photograph for her role in *Orphans of the Storm,* her last film made with Griffith. Soon after the movie's completion, Griffith urged her to approach other moviemakers for parts because he could not pay her what she was worth.

# Lillian Gish
1893–1993
*Actress*

ALFRED CHENEY
JOHNSTON
(1885–1971)
Gelatin silver print
33 × 25.5 cm (13 × 10⅟₁₆ in.)
1922

By her late teens, Doris Humphrey had set her sights on a performing career in dance. Unfortunately, following graduation from high school in 1913, she found herself having to support her parents as a ballroom dance instructor. In the summer of 1917, however, she attended a session at the Denishawn School in Los Angeles, whose founders, Ruth St. Denis and Ted Shawn, were creating new dance forms based on Middle Eastern and Asian traditions. St. Denis recognized Humphrey's promise immediately, and Humphrey soon joined the school as both teacher and performer in its company.

In 1928, Humphrey teamed up with another Denishawn dancer, Charles Weidman, and they formed their own dance company. Over the next several years, Humphrey began evolving a dance vocabulary premised on the conviction that dance was, above all, an expression of emotion. Among the Humphrey-Weidman Company's finest moments was the staging in the mid-1930s of Humphrey's trilogy of compositions, *New Dance*, *Theatre Piece*, and *With My Red Fires*, which represented the most ambitious and demanding modern dance enterprise yet mounted.

Arthritis ended Humphrey's performing career in the mid-1940s, but she continued to work as a choreographer. In 1951, she joined the faculty of the Juilliard School of Music, where she once told a class that a dancer "never stops wondering at [the] infinite possibilities" of movement. When she died, the *New York Times* critic John Martin declared that her contribution to American dance was as enduring "as the granite under the soil."

This photograph was taken when Humphrey was still performing with the Denishawn Dance Company. In it, she wears a wig of simulated seaweed that was part of her costume in Ruth St. Denis's ballet *The Spirit of the Sea*.

# Doris Humphrey

1895–1958

*Dancer*

NICKOLAS MURAY
(1892–1965)
Gelatin silver print
24.6 × 19.2 cm (9 $^{11}/_{16}$ × 7 $^{9}/_{16}$ in.)
circa 1923

Recalling his first sight of dancer Josephine Baker in the musical *Shuffle Along* in the early 1920s, poet Langston Hughes remarked that "there was something about her rhythm, her warmth, her smile, and her impudent grace that made her stand out." Indeed, whenever she set foot on stage, her comic verve and easy sensuality made her the center of attention, no matter how many others were there with her. Even so, when Baker went to Paris in 1925 to perform in *La Revue Nègre*, no one could have anticipated her electric impact on the city. The moment the opening-night audience saw her, writer Janet Flanner noted, "a scream of salutation" went up, and "within a half hour of the final curtain ... the news of her arrival ... had spread to the cafes on the Champs-Elysées."

When *La Revue Nègre* went to Berlin, the response to Baker was much the same. On her return to Paris, she was soon ensconced as a star of the Folies-Bergère, where she introduced the French to the Charleston and danced in a G-string decorated with bananas. By 1927, she had received some forty thousand love letters and many hundreds of marriage proposals. Picasso proclaimed Baker the "Nefertiti of now," while the writer Colette declared her a "beautiful panther." She also captivated haute-couture designers, who supplied her with free clothes, thinking that her slim, light-brown body was the ideal vehicle for showing off their wares.

This photograph depicts Baker in her first revue at the Folies-Bergère in 1926. In the dance number pictured here, she reached the stage concealed in a flowered ball lowered from above. Once the ball hit the stage, it slowly opened, revealing a scantily clad Baker on a large mirror that became her dancing surface. The audience loved it.

# Josephine Baker
1906–1975
*Dancer, singer*

STANISLAUS J. WALERY
(active 1880s–1920s)
Gelatin silver print
22.2 × 16.2 cm (8¾ × 6⅜ in.)
1926

Novelist Willa Cather regarded her family's move in 1883 from Virginia to the Nebraska frontier as the most wrenching experience of her life. Upon encountering the vast, treeless expanses of the Nebraska plains, so different from the rolling, verdant terrain of Virginia, she felt as if she were undergoing "an erasure of personality." It was a trauma she never fully got over. Nevertheless, Cather came to see the pioneer life of the Great Plains as a repository of cherished values, and it was that life that became the primary source for her fiction.

While writing her first Great Plains novel, *O Pioneers!*, Cather harbored no great hopes for popular interest in this story "set in Nebraska of all places!" But a story set in Nebraska did have interest after all—at least when it was told by Cather. At the book's publication in 1913, one critic proclaimed it to be "touched with genius."

Cather's period of greatest acclaim began with the appearance in 1922 of her Pulitzer Prize–winning novel *One of Ours*, which was soon followed by the much-praised *A Lost Lady*. But her greatest triumph came in 1927, with the publication of her tale of two French missionary priests in the Southwest, *Death Comes for the Archbishop*. The book inspired an avalanche of rave reviews, including one declaring it the ultimate fruition of Cather's "literary artistry" and "an American classic."

Just before that triumph, *Vanity Fair* ran this portrait of Cather with a caption hailing her as "a stylist of precision and beauty." Several months later, following the appearance of *Death Comes for the Archbishop*, the magazine published yet another likeness of her. This time, the caption declared her "heir apparent to Edith Wharton's lonely eminence among America's women novelists."

# Willa Cather
1873–1947
*Writer*

EDWARD STEICHEN
(1879–1973)
Gelatin silver print
24 × 19.2 cm (9⁷⁄₁₆ × 7⁹⁄₁₆ in.), 1927
Acquired in memory of Agnes and Eugene Meyer through the generosity of Katharine Graham and the New York Community Trust, The Island Fund

Malvina Hoffman studied painting for six years. But when it came to doing her father's likeness in 1909, she felt the need to depict him in three dimensions. Laying her brushes aside, she tried modeling his features in clay. In the process, the aspiring painter became an aspiring sculptor, and in 1910, Hoffman was on her way to Paris, where she convinced a reluctant Auguste Rodin to accept her as a student.

During her Paris stay, Hoffman became an habitué of the Ballets Russes, which instilled an abiding concern for movement in her work. Nowhere was that more evident than in her first artistic triumph, *Bacchanale Russe*, a high-spirited composition portraying dancers Anna Pavlova and Mikhail Mordkin. Hoffman once wondered if her lack of interest in modernism "might not be a defect." But that self-doubt was short-lived. Her art remained rooted in the representational tradition, and among her finest pieces were her naturalistic portraits.

The Yugoslavian sculptor Ivan Meštrović once warned Hoffman that to command respect within her overwhelmingly male profession, she might have to exceed the norm in mastering physical and mechanical aspects of her art that were generally left to others. Sometimes she heeded the advice more than was wise. Poet Marianne Moore remembered a time in London in the mid-1920s when Hoffman was overseeing the installation of her two huge stone figures symbolizing Britain and America. Once they were installed in their lofty setting, Hoffman noted a need for slight modification, and she was soon some 90 feet (27 m) in the air, making alterations with her mallet and chisel. It was, Moore said, "as if she had wings and carried a torch."

In this photograph, Hoffman stands before her larger-than-life, full-length likeness of her friend Meštrović, who had recently offered her instruction in modeling animals.

# Malvina Hoffman
1885–1966
*Sculptor*

CLARA E. SIPPRELL
(1885–1975)
Gelatin silver print
23.2 × 19 cm (9⅛ × 7½ in.)
circa 1928

In late December 1921, an aspiring writer named Ernest Hemingway walked into a combination bookshop–lending library on Paris's Left Bank. It was love at first sight. The shop was called Shakespeare and Company, and with its wide-ranging fare of English-language books, it was just the sort of place that a young writer, still in search of his own literary voice, was bound to like.

The shop's proprietor was Sylvia Beach, daughter of an American Presbyterian minister. Originally her clientele had been mostly French. But, by the time of Hemingway's first visit, the shop had become a center for the Anglo-American modernist writers who flocked to Paris after World War I, among them John Dos Passos, Ezra Pound, and Ford Madox Ford.

Beach's place in Anglo-American letters, however, goes well beyond her role as a bookshop proprietor. In 1921, when it became clear that the sexual frankness of James Joyce's *Ulysses* precluded its publication in the United States or the British Isles, Beach undertook management of the novel's publication in France, and on February 2, 1922, the first bound copies of the work arrived at her shop. For the next eleven years, Beach continued to oversee new editions of this watershed novel and to cater to the wants of its often difficult author.

Beach's shop featured a photographic gallery of the Anglo-American writers who congregated at Shakespeare and Company. Among the photographers supplying the pictures was Berenice Abbott, who took this likeness, showing Beach clad in a shiny slickerlike coat. The image's cool, hard-edged quality is suggestive of a personality that was all practicality and no sentiment. In fact, Beach was just the opposite. If it was a choice between looking out for her own interest and doing a kindness for a patron, the latter inevitably won out.

# Sylvia Beach
## 1887–1962
## *Publisher, bookseller*

BERENICE ABBOTT
(1898–1991)
Gelatin silver print
9.5 × 8 cm (3¾ × 3⅛ in.)
1928

Berenice Abbott went to Paris in 1921 intending to become a sculptor. By late 1923, however, she had concluded that sculpture was not for her. During this period of uncertainty, she ran into photographer Man Ray, who mentioned that he needed a darkroom assistant. "How about me?" offered Abbott. With that, her career in photography was launched.

At Man Ray's studio, Abbott's activities were initially confined to printing and developing. But in her second year, she began taking pictures of her own. Remembering her first moments with a camera, she claimed, "I had no idea of becoming a photographer, but the pictures kept coming out." Better yet, "most of them were good." By 1926, she was establishing her own studio, specializing in portraiture. Among her sitters were such noted literary figures as Jean Cocteau, André Maurois, and James Joyce.

But as the literati paraded past Abbott's camera, the seeds were being sown for a new phase in her photographic career. Long fascinated with Eugène Atget's photographs of Paris, Abbott befriended Atget and acquired his picture archive following his death in 1927. The new trove of photographs whetted Abbott's appetite for a shift in emphasis in her own work, and in 1929 she moved to New York City, hoping to create an urban chronicle comparable to Atget's. Want of money initially got in the way. But finally, with backing from the New Deal's Federal Art Project, her hopes for documenting New York were realized. And like Atget, she infused her record of time and place with an immediacy that continues to entrance present-day viewers.

Abbott's self-portrait from her early days in New York evinces the unforced objectivity that was a trademark of her portraiture.

# Berenice Abbott
1898–1991
*Photographer*

SELF-PORTRAIT
Gelatin silver print
14.1 × 10.9 cm (5⁹⁄₁₆ × 4¼ in.)
circa 1932

The daughter of missionaries, Pearl Buck spent most of her childhood in China, and by her late teens, her feel for the country's culture ran as deep, if not deeper, than her knowledge of her native United States. As a young woman married to an agricultural missionary, she continued to live mostly in China. So, as Buck embarked on her writing career in the early 1920s, her focus on that country was almost inevitable.

Buck's first writings on China were nonfiction magazine articles. But by the late 1920s, she was trying her hand at fiction, and in 1930, a pairing of two of her stories, entitled *East Wind: West Wind*, reached print. The book sold well, but it was soon overshadowed by Buck's novel, *The Good Earth*. Borrowing its narrative tone from Chinese storytelling, this tale of a Chinese couple's rise to wealth became a bestseller almost instantly, claimed a Pulitzer Prize, and was made into both a play and a movie. In presenting Buck with its Howells Medal in 1935, the American Academy of Arts and Letters declared *The Good Earth* "the most distinguished work of American fiction" of the past five years.

In 1936, following two sequels to *The Good Earth*, Buck published *The Exile* and *Fighting Angel*, which recounted the missionary lives of her mother and father. The ultimate accolade for these two books came in 1938, when they were specially singled out for praise in the citation awarding Buck the Nobel Prize in literature.

The Nobel Prize represented the high-water mark of Buck's career. Nevertheless, her later books continued to bear witness to her remarkable talent for engaging narrative.

*Vanity Fair* featured this portrait of Buck in its November 1932 issue, in a picture spread titled "Nominated for the Hall of Fame: 1932."

# Pearl S. Buck
1892–1973
*Writer*

EDWARD STEICHEN
(1879–1973)
Gelatin silver print
24.8 × 19.6 cm (9¾ × 7¹¹/₁₆ in.)
1932

When it came to "looks, grace, and carriage," *Vanity Fair* reported in September 1932, the U.S. women's swim team at the recent Los Angeles summer Olympics boasted "five angels" worthy of "a Ziegfeld chorus." As proof of that assertion, the magazine offered a full-page reproduction of this photograph by Edward Steichen of Eleanor Holm (standing) and Helene Madison (seated).

Beauty, however, was the least of these two young women's stories. Between 1927 and 1936, Holm claimed thirty-five U.S. swimming championships, and at the Los Angeles games, she easily won the gold medal in the hundred-meter backstroke. More impressive yet was the evidence of Helene Madison's athletic prowess. From 1928 to the end of her swimming career, Madison never lost a freestyle race of any distance. When the Associated Press named her female athlete of the year in late 1931, she could lay claim to ten world freestyle records, and at the Olympics the following year, she became the second female swimmer to win three gold medals. When she retired from competition not long after, she held three Olympic records, forty-five American records, and seventeen world records.

*Vanity Fair* noted that Madison was too much the unrelenting competitor to be well liked among her fellow swimmers, but once in the water, she invited only admiration. There, she became "a human torpedo boat gliding forward, smoothly, steadily and relentlessly with such a sense of power and rhythm" that it made one "exult to watch her."

Steichen's picture of Holm and Madison offers a good demonstration of the brilliant sense of design that underlay so much of his work, and testifies to what one critic called his "uncanny ability to manipulate reality" for his own aesthetic ends.

---

# Eleanor Holm
1913–2004
# Helene Madison
1913–1970
*Athletes*

EDWARD STEICHEN
(1879–1973)
Gelatin silver print
24.1 × 19.3 cm (9½ × 7⅝ in.), 1932
Acquired in memory of Agnes and Eugene Meyer through the generosity of Katharine Graham and the New York Community Trust, The Island Fund

When Katharine Hepburn struck her pose for this likeness by Edward Steichen in late 1933, she was riding a crest. The previous year, her Broadway performance in *The Warrior's Husband* had earned her a generous contract with RKO studios, and in her first movie, *A Bill of Divorcement*, she amply demonstrated her worth, as critics singled out her performance as one of the film's main virtues. Hard on the heels of that success came an Academy Award–winning portrayal of an aspiring actress in *Morning Glory*, and the release of RKO's widely praised *Little Women*, in which Hepburn played Jo March.

As Steichen refined the lighting for her likeness, Hepburn was about to return to Broadway in *The Lake*, and it was in anticipation that this too would prove a triumph that Steichen shot this image for *Vanity Fair*. Unfortunately, the play flopped dreadfully. Writing in *Vanity Fair* a month after Steichen's portrait appeared, critic George Nathan opined: "Miss Hepburn … may one day" become an "actress of position.… But that day … is still far from being at hand."

Over the next several years. Hepburn's career lost its momentum. By the late 1930s, the mediocrity of many of her movies, along with her difficult ways, had made her box-office poison. By the spring of 1939, however, she was about to start riding yet another crest, as Tracy Lord in the Broadway production of *The Philadelphia Story*. Critic Brooks Atkinson wrote that Hepburn played the strong-willed Lord "like a woman who has at last found the joy she has always been seeking in the theater." In effect, she had become "an actress of position," and it was an eminence that would only grow with the years.

# Katharine Hepburn
1907–2003
*Actress*

EDWARD STEICHEN
(1879–1973)
Gelatin silver print
23.2 × 19.4 cm (9⅛ × 7⅝ in.)
1933

A succession of stellar athletes made the 1920s a golden era in American sports, and in women's tennis the star's name was Helen Wills Moody. Nicknamed "Little Miss Poker Face," the tightly controlled Moody was not exciting to watch and did not generate roars of enthusiasm. But while Moody's style left many fans cold, it led to an indisputably impressive record.

Beginning in 1923, Moody dominated women's tennis for more than a decade. The top-ranked women's player over eight successive years, she eventually claimed thirty-one grand-slam titles. By the time she retired in 1938, her triumphs included eight British singles championships, four French, and seven American.

An impressive string of victories was not Moody's only legacy to tennis. With her short-skirted playing outfits, she also helped free women's tennis from the fetters of Victorian convention. More important, however, it was the toughness of Moody's playing that sparked the transformation of women's tennis from a decorative sideshow into a rigorously competitive enterprise.

Moody is pictured playing in the U.S. Women's National Singles Championship of 1933, where she faced Helen Jacobs in the final match. The outcome of the Moody–Jacobs face-off seemed a foregone conclusion. The best that Jacobs had ever done against Moody was win three games in one set. But Jacobs surprised everyone in the U.S. final by taking the first set, 8–6. In the next set, Moody came back to win 6–3. Then, in the decisive third set, Jacobs took the lead quickly. But before Jacobs could bring home her all-but-certain triumph, Moody exited the court, pleading severe pain and leaving Jacobs the winner by default. Some argued that, whether in pain or not, Moody owed it to Jacobs to finish the match. But "Little Miss Poker Face," true to her reputation, had no comment.

# Helen Wills Moody
## 1905–1998
### Athlete

By an unidentified photographer
for Acme Newspictures, Inc.
Gelatin silver print
16.9 × 21.4 cm (6 ¹¹/₁₆ × 8 ⁷/₁₆ in.)
1933

Looking at the scowling face in this picture, it would surprise no one to learn that this is a woman who never shied away from controversy. But to say that Emma Goldman relished controversy hardly does her justice. Known as "Red Emma," she was the quintessential political radical—extreme, unrelenting, and fearless.

Born in Russia, Goldman immigrated to the United States in 1885 and settled in Rochester, New York, where her work in a factory quickly soured her on American capitalism. By 1890, she had embraced anarchism, calling for replacement of the state with egalitarian communes, and in promoting her cause, she saw nothing wrong with a little lawbreaking. During the Homestead Strike of 1892, she collaborated in a failed attempt to assassinate Carnegie Steel executive Henry Clay Frick, and the following year she went to prison for telling unemployed workers that it was their right to steal food.

Goldman's vision of an anarchistic paradise was far too extreme to draw much of a following. Nevertheless, many of the specific causes that she championed, such as better working conditions and women's rights, were also espoused by more moderate reformers. But she was ever the radical at heart and for years was regarded as one of the most dangerous extremists in America. In 1919, after serving a term in prison for opposing military conscription during World War I, she was deported to her native Russia.

When Goldman was allowed to return to the United States for ninety days in 1934, a journalist asked her if time had softened her views. "No," she answered, "I was always considered bad; I'm worse now." To another reporter who asked if she thought she was reasonable, she said, "Who the hell wants to be reasonable?"

# Emma Goldman
## 1869–1940
### *Reformer*

CARL VAN VECHTEN
(1880–1964)
Gelatin silver print
25.2 × 20.1 cm (9¹⁵/₁₆ × 7¹⁵/₁₆ in.)
1934
Gift of Virginia M. Zabriskie

PHOTOGRAPH BY
CARL VAN VECHTEN

No one ever ranked Mae West among Hollywood's most significant acting talents or included her among its great screen beauties. Still, there was something compelling in her hand-on-hip earthiness, and her sly portrayals of worldly wise sirens remain some of the most memorable moments in American moviemaking.

West developed the ingredients of her racy persona in vaudeville and New York revues. On occasion, indignation over the suggestiveness of her act got her into trouble. But she remained unchastened, and by the mid-1920s, West was applying her gifts for the risqué to creating plays she could star in. Her first effort, entitled *Sex*, proved a box-office hit. Its raciness, however, forced its closure and landed West in jail, and her only major success at playwriting was *Diamond Lil*, in which she starred as the loose woman with a heart of gold.

When West went to Hollywood in the early 1930s, her vamp's persona translated well to the screen. In 1933, her *I'm No Angel* and *She Done Him Wrong* were two of the year's biggest hits, and she soon ranked among Hollywood's most highly paid performers.

Perhaps the most enduring aspect of West's career is the host of suggestive one-liners that have become catchphrases in American pop culture. Easily the most familiar is "Come up and see me some time," from *Diamond Lil*. Almost as famous is her confession that "between two evils I always pick the one I never tried before."

This photograph was among the publicity images for the movie *Goin' to Town*, released in 1935. Unfortunately, owing partly to an attempt to placate Hollywood's censors, the film lacked the usual West verve. "What once looked like hearty bawdiness," said one critic, had been reduced to mere "handwriting on the back fence."

---

# Mae West
1893–1980
*Actress*

C. KENNETH LOBBEN
(circa 1905–1961)
Gelatin silver print
31.7 × 24.3 cm (12½ × 9⁹⁄₁₆ in.)
1935
Gift of Keith de Lellis

It is almost axiomatic that anyone starting out in professional dance past the age of twenty should not expect to go very far. Enrolling in her first dance class at twenty-two, Martha Graham proved a notable exception. The founder of her own dance company, Graham performed until she was seventy-five. Along the way, she choreographed more than 180 original works and became the preeminent figure in creating modern dance.

Seeking to engender a visceral response from her audiences, Graham premised her dance on the idea that formal movement should grow out of emotion. When she started working out that principle in dance compositions, she met with a good deal of hostility that continued for years. Summing up one of her performances, one reviewer wrote, "Ugly girl makes ugly movements onstage, while ugly mother tells ugly brother to make ugly sounds on drum." Another critic, however, who shared that view, acknowledged that by the mid-1930s there was a growing body of Graham adherents who were liable to respond to his negativism with "letters comparing him, unfavorably, with Ivan the Terrible."

Graham had her first great public success in 1938 with *American Document*, a re-creation in dance of moments from America's past. Two years later, her *Letter to the World*, inspired by the poetry of Emily Dickinson, was hailed as "a miracle of intuition." Her most widely celebrated work, however, was *Appalachian Spring*, a compelling celebration of America's rustic heritage first staged in 1944 to music by Aaron Copland.

This likeness dates from late March 1936, when Graham's company was performing in San Francisco. Of those who were still finding her work too avant-garde, she had recently declared, "No artist is ahead of his time.... It is just that the others are behind the time."

# Martha Graham
## 1894–1991
### *Dancer, choreographer*

SONYA NOSKOWIAK
(1900–1975)
Gelatin silver print
21.8 × 16.7 cm (8 ⁹⁄₁₆ × 6 ⁹⁄₁₆ in.)
circa 1936

When Amelia Earhart took her first plane ride in 1920, it was love at first sight. Whatever the hazards of this new mode of travel, she was determined to pilot a plane herself. On January 3, 1921, she took her first flying lesson, and the following summer, she bought her own plane. By late 1922, she was setting a new women's altitude record of 14,000 feet (4,270 m), and over the next few years she became a familiar figure at air shows.

Aviation, however, could not provide Earhart with the living that she needed, and by 1927, the year Charles Lindbergh made his historic nonstop Atlantic flight, she was working at a Boston settlement house. Then, in the spring of 1928, flying again became her chief preoccupation, when she was invited to become the first woman to cross the North Atlantic on a nonstop flight. On June 18, when the plane landed in Wales, Earhart was suddenly one of the most celebrated aviators in the world. Charmed by her fresh, wholesome presence, the public embraced her as Lindbergh's female counterpart, "Lady Lindy." More important, the flight opened the way for other flying opportunities, and in 1932, she became the first woman to pilot a solo nonstop flight across the Atlantic.

In this picture, Earhart is perched in the unfinished fuselage of the Lockheed Electra that was to be her "flying laboratory" in a flight around the world. Earhart and navigator Fred Noonan took off in the plane from Miami, Florida, on June 1, 1937. In early July, with the journey more than half over, their plane disappeared somewhere in the South Pacific. To this day, the exact circumstances of that disappearance remain one of the great mysteries in aviation history.

# Amelia Earhart
1897–1937
*Aviator*

By an unidentified photographer
for International News Photos
Gelatin silver print
20.8 × 15.8 cm (8⁹⁄₁₆ × 6⁵⁄₁₆ in.)
1936

Dressed as the young Queen Victoria for the play *Victoria Regina*, actress Helen Hayes stands in this picture at the height of her long career. In this drama spanning Victoria's entire reign, the thirty-five-year-old Hayes faced the task of depicting a woman from her late teens to enfeebled old age, and she might have been forgiven if some aspects of her multiaged portrayal proved less convincing than others. But forgiveness was never even an issue. From beginning to end, Hayes invested her performance with a credibility that has long been considered one of the finest moments in Broadway history. As Victoria, observed one critic, she "re-creates not only a monarch but an age."

Hayes, however, had not always seemed destined for such admiration. She was a seasoned actress by 1920, but by no means a great one. As the lead in *Bab* that year, reviewers found her shrill and artificial, and in the wake of continuing negative reviews in other roles, Hayes was soon pursuing all manner of instruction to improve her credibility—from voice lessons to fencing to interpretative dancing.

The effort paid off. By 1927, when Hayes opened in *Coquette*, it was clear that she had matured into a first-rank talent. On opening night, the play's producer, Jed Harris, recalled that he had never "seen anything like the ovation Miss Hayes received."

Hayes strikes a pose in this picture from the first scene in *Victoria Regina*, when the nineteen-year-old Victoria is called from her bed to be told that her uncle, King William IV, is dead and that she is now Britain's queen. This was the first magic moment of the play in which, according to *Time*, Hayes "by some alchemy of gesture and expression" managed to "convey in full" her character's simultaneous sense of bewilderment and delight.

# Helen Hayes
1900–1993
*Actress*

ALFREDO VALENTE
(1899–1973)
Gelatin silver print
32.6 × 22.7 cm (12¹³⁄₁₆ × 8¹⁵⁄₁₆ in.)
1936

Blessed with a luminous complexion once likened to a "rose blushing through ivory," Anna May Wong had the distinction in 1922 of claiming the female lead in Hollywood's first Technicolor movie, *The Toll of the Sea*. With her performance two years later as a Mongol slave in the box-office smash *The Thief of Bagdad*, she became the movie industry's leading Chinese American actress. But that was quite different from being a leading actress of Caucasian origin. Because of prevailing popular prejudices, Wong never had a chance for the best parts, even when the character was Asian.

In 1928, Wong went to Europe, where she was able to play the lead roles that had routinely been denied her in America. Still, the tolerance there also had its limits. In 1929, when her film *The Road to Dishonour* opened in England, censors ordered her kisses with the Caucasian leading man cut from the film.

In 1931, Wong returned to the United States, pretty much reconciled now to playing lesser roles. Nevertheless, when casting began for the film based on Pearl S. Buck's novel *The Good Earth*, she had her heart set on winning the Chinese female lead. Instead, the part went to Caucasian actress Luise Rainer. Doubtless compounding Wong's bitterness over not getting the role was the fact that Rainer won an Oscar for it.

When Wong posed for this picture, the most active part of her screen career was nearing its close. Most likely it was taken in New York in the spring of 1937, when she was performing Chinese songs and sketches at a theater there. Despite past experience, she was harboring hopes of landing a choice Asian part in the upcoming *Adventures of Marco Polo*, but as usual, it went to someone else.

# Anna May Wong
## 1905–1961
### *Actress*

NICKOLAS MURAY
(1892–1965)
Color carbro print
39 × 31.1 cm (15⅜ × 12¼ in.)
1937

In this photograph, fashion designer Elizabeth Hawes seems poised to press a typewriter key, thus causing her right hand to plunge a pin into a dress form. In other words, she seems on the verge of subjecting her profession to some discomfiting, voodoolike torture. No image better sums up a central strand of Hawes's fashion odyssey.

Hawes started her fashion career in Paris, working for a concern that pirated dress designs from haute-couture salons. By the time she turned to reporting on French high fashion for the *New Yorker* in early 1927, her cynicism about the industry had taken firm root. Signing her articles "Parasite," she wasted no time in attacking high fashion's tyranny over women. In one instance, her column opened with the tongue-in-cheek cable assertion, "ALL REDDISH BROWN OR BLACK PRINTS ARE SMART CHANEL SAYS SO IT MUST BE SO."

After returning to America in 1928, Hawes built a considerable reputation as a designer of elegant clothes that were both comfortable and flattering. Success, however, did not kill her impulse to criticize her industry. In 1938, she published *Fashion Is Spinach*, in which she lamented the power of French couturiers to make women feel "absolutely out of fashion" if they failed, for example, to have two silver foxes hanging around their necks. She declared the whole notion of fashion "a complete anachronism."

In 1940, Hawes closed her New York salon to write a column for the newspaper *PM*, and a few years later became involved in advancing the concerns of women in the labor force. But ultimately she returned to fashion, reopening her New York salon for a short time in the late 1940s. In 1954, she came out with *It's Still Spinach*, in which she once again waxed eloquent on the tyranny of fashion-world dictates.

# Elizabeth Hawes
## 1903–1971
*Fashion designer*

RALPH STEINER
(1899–1986)
Gelatin silver print
18.9 × 24.1 cm (7⁷⁄₁₆ × 9⁹⁄₁₆ in.)
circa 1938

"Boom in Child Stars" ran a headline in *Time* in mid-1938, and to substantiate that assertion, the magazine reeled off a list of youngsters who were currently in great demand in Hollywood, among them Freddie Bartholomew, Jane Withers, and Judy Garland. But there was one star who eclipsed them all. Her name was Shirley Temple, and for the previous three years, this dimpled bundle of unrelenting effervescence had been the movie industry's top box-office draw.

In the mostly forgettable *Stand Up and Cheer!*, Temple had wowed audiences early in 1934 with her song-and-dance rendition of "Baby Take a Bow." Fox Studios, however, with which she had a contract, was not quick to grasp the impact of that performance. Instead of finding its own showcase for her talents, it lent her out to Paramount. But by year's end, the message had been absorbed. With Temple's performances in Paramount's *Little Miss Marker* and Fox's *Bright Eyes* about to earn her a special Oscar for her outstanding contribution to movie entertainment, it was clear that she was one of Hollywood's hottest properties.

Temple was also one of Hollywood's easiest stars to work with. She often knew the script so well that she could supply forgotten lines to other cast members. At one rehearsal, she mastered five dance numbers simply by listening to the feet of her dance partner, "Bojangles" Robinson.

In mid-June 1938, in anticipation of Temple's visit to New York City, the *New York Daily News* featured this image on the cover of its photogravure section. Some easterners expressed disgust with all the attention that the press gave to her visit. To the naysayers, the *New York Times* replied: "Shame on them! Shirley belongs in the very spot into which she has hurled herself—right in the great big, soft-shelled heart of America."

# Shirley Temple
born 1928
*Actress*

HARRY WARNECKE
(1900–1984)
and Lee Elkins (lifedates unknown)
Color carbro print
42.5 × 32.8 cm (16⅗ × 12¹³⁄₁₆ in.)
1938
Gift of Elsie M. Warnecke

Described on her death as the "voice of American fashion," Carmel Snow began advancing toward that distinction working as an assistant in her mother's custom dressmaking salon in New York City. In 1921, she became an assistant fashion editor at *Vogue* and within eight years was chief editor of its American edition. In 1932, she accepted a demotion to become fashion editor at *Harper's Bazaar*, a flagging competitor that had defied recent efforts to revitalize its tired pages.

*Harper's Bazaar* was not as hopeless as it looked, at least in the hands of Snow, who became its editor-in-chief in 1935. One of her earliest contributions to the magazine's revival was the enlistment of a sports photographer to photograph models in bathing suits running down a beach. The result was a spread of in situ fashion shots that soon became one of the magazine's most engaging trademarks. Equally momentous was Snow's hiring of Alexey Brodovitch as art director in 1934, which led to *Harper's Bazaar* becoming a pacesetter in magazine design.

As *Harper's Bazaar* thrived, Snow's stature as a fashion arbiter became formidable, and her mere appearance at a dress-collection showing was enough to send a designer's spirits soaring. "You can't keep an exciting fashion down," she once said. Still, as such designers as Dior and Balenciaga well knew, it never hurt to have Snow in one's corner.

The maker of this portrait, George Hoyningen-Huene, was one of Snow's earliest recruiting coups for *Harper's Bazaar*. A gifted and innovative fashion photographer, Hoyningen-Huene had worked for *Vogue* for many years. But one afternoon in 1935, he quit in a huff and telephoned Snow to offer his services. Snow knew that Hoyningen-Huene could be very difficult, but she made him an offer anyway, thus snagging one of her competition's greatest assets.

# Carmel Snow
1887–1961
*Editor, fashion arbiter*

GEORGE HOYNINGEN-HUENE
(1900–1968)
Gelatin silver print
27.6 × 21.8 cm (10⅞ × 8⁹⁄₁₆ in.)
1939

Katharine Cornell once confessed that her stage fright "got worse as the years went on." On days when she had an evening performance, she said, "I don't think … that I was ever happy—beginning at 4 o'clock any afternoon." Those may seem to be strange recollections coming from a seasoned actress. Nevertheless, they were quite genuine, and Cornell's illustrious career is perhaps the ultimate proof of the constructive potential of stage fright. As critic Brooks Atkinson once put it, every time she stepped on to the stage, "something electric happened."

Cornell made her first significant splash in 1919, when she appeared in London as Jo March in a stage version of *Little Women*, but over the next several years, she appeared in a succession of mostly undistinguished plays. In late 1924, however, she landed a lead role in a play worthy of her talents, George Bernard Shaw's *Candida*. Her performance, which one critic said "had something in it of the light of another world," marked the first step toward becoming a legend of the American stage.

Final consolidation of that legend began six years later, when Cornell bought the production rights for *The Barretts of Wimpole Street* as a gift for her director husband, Guthrie McClintic. Cornell did not think she was appropriate for the female lead of Elizabeth Barrett Browning, but her husband persuaded her otherwise. In early 1931, the play opened in New York to rave reviews that hailed Cornell as, among other things, "an actress of the first order."

Cornell is pictured here as the female lead in a 1941 production of Shaw's *Doctor's Dilemma*. The artist, Louise Dahl-Wolfe, worked at *Harper's Bazaar* for many years, producing fashion and celebrity photographs that were widely admired for their innovative composition.

# Katharine Cornell
1893–1974
*Actress*

LOUISE DAHL-WOLFE
(1895–1989)
Gelatin silver print
28 × 27.1 cm (11 × 10¹¹/₁₆ in.)
1941

In the press coverage of World War II, some of the correspondents charged with reporting the war became news items in themselves. Perhaps the best case in point was *Life* photographer Margaret Bourke-White. In mid-1941, *Life* deemed her success in finagling a photo session with the reclusive Joseph Stalin sufficiently newsworthy to make it a feature story. In late 1942, she again became part of her own photo story when, on her way to the African front, her boat was sunk by a German torpedo. Not long afterward, she became the first woman allowed to go on a combat flying mission, and when *Life* ran the resulting pictures, the headline read "Life's Margaret Bourke-White Goes Bombing." In short, when it came to newsworthiness, Bourke-White sometimes ranked right up there with the generals.

Bourke-White's reputation, however, did not rest just on her wartime exclusives. Beginning in 1936, her pictures had helped establish *Life*'s preeminence in the art of the photographic essay. Further adding to her reputation were her evocative images of southern sharecropper poverty in *You Have Seen Their Faces*, a collaboration with writer Erskine Caldwell that became a classic in photographic reportage. When *U.S. Camera* declared her "the most famous on-the-spot reporter the world over" in 1940, the claim seemed well justified.

Bourke-White's fame, however, by no means guaranteed that all her photographic ventures would be unalloyed triumphs. Not long after posing for this photograph in New York, she went back to covering the war, this time in Italy, where, in her own estimation, she shot some of her finest work. Unfortunately, military censors lost the best of those pictures. Recalling the incident years later, Bourke-White observed, "It does no good when wisecrackers remark, 'Anything can happen in the Pentagon.' The wound remains unhealed."

# Margaret Bourke-White
## 1906–1971
*Photographer*

PHILIPPE HALSMAN
(1906–1979)
Gelatin silver print
35.8 × 26.8 cm (14¹⁄₈ × 10¹⁄₂ in.)
1943
Gift of Irène Halsman

Dorothy Parker's friend Alexander Woollcott once called her a "blend of Little Nell and Lady Macbeth." As Parker clutches herself here at age fifty, the camera seems to have captured the Little Nell part of that blend.

But the public perceptions of this critic, poet, and short-story writer tilted more in the direction of Lady Macbeth. Figuratively at least, Parker's sharp wit could be as lethal as any Scottish regicide's dagger, and as a member of New York's legendary Algonquin Round Table of literati in the 1920s, she enjoyed a celebrity built largely on her gift for coining devastating barbs and sardonic bon mots. To a young man who once said that he could not abide fools, she mused, "That's queer. Your mother could." As for her own epitaph, she wanted it to read "Excuse my dust."

A staff book reviewer for the *New Yorker*, Parker also produced a good deal of poetry—best remembered for its blend of tragic perceptions and jaded wisecracks—and in the 1930s, she tried screenwriting. The most enduring feature of her output, however, were her short stories, the best of which have been compared favorably to the work of Ring Lardner and Ernest Hemingway.

The sense of vulnerability apparent in Parker's likeness of 1943 was probably no accident. Beneath her wisecracking exterior, she had always been fundamentally insecure, and with the most productive part of her career over, it may have been inevitable that any picture of Parker at this stage would be less than ebullient. Nevertheless, Parker could still turn a witty phrase. Musing on being over fifty, she observed that there was no need to lie about her age anymore. After all, she said, "What's a couple of sandspits to an archipelago?"

# Dorothy Parker
1893–1967
*Writer*

GEORGE PLATT LYNES
(1907–1955)
Gelatin silver print
22.8 × 19 cm (9 × 7 ½ in.)
1943

After graduating from Hunter College in 1940, Pearl Primus intended to become a physician. However, when she sought to finance her medical schooling as a laboratory technician, she found that such opportunities were closed to African Americans. Instead, she found a job working in wardrobe at a dance group. On being made an understudy in the group, Primus suddenly found she had an extraordinary gift for dancing, and within two years, dance had become her full-time vocation. By then she had also begun to focus on using dance to dramatize the black American experience.

At her professional debut in 1943, Primus's program featured *African Ceremonial*, a piece inspired by her studies of African culture, and *Strange Fruit*, a composition focused on America's mob lynchings of blacks. The thematic content and quality of Primus's performance proved a compelling meld. One critic effused: "If ever a young dancer was entitled to a company of her own ... she is it."

Primus is seen in this photograph performing yet another of her compositions from her premier concert, *Hard Times Blues*, a piece that evoked the harsh realities of southern black sharecropping. Her stiff-necked, contorted stance in the picture hints at the vigorous athleticism of her style. As *Time* put it several years later, "Her forte is force."

Forming her own dance troupe in 1944, Primus went on to study firsthand the dance traditions of Africa and of West Indian blacks and, in the process, greatly enriched her own compositions. Eventually earning a doctorate in anthropology, she had a profound influence on several generations of African American dancers. As for what her career meant to her, Primus once said, "Dance is my medicine.... [It] is the fist with which I fight the sickening ignorance of prejudice."

# Pearl Primus
1919–1994
*Dancer, choreographer*

LISETTE MODEL
(1901–1983)
Gelatin silver print
27.6 × 34.7 cm (10⅞ × 13¹¹/₁₆ in.)
1943

When *Life* magazine ran a photo spread in late 1943 depicting a late-night jam session of New York jazz musicians, the caption beneath this image of pianist Mary Lou Williams described her as "one of the very few capable female jazz musicians." That description hardly did justice to Williams. As both performer and composer, she was not merely "capable"; she was superb. "If you shut your eyes," noted one admirer, "you would bet she was a man." In an age that still harbored doubts about women's fitness for so many endeavors, this was high praise indeed, especially in an art form that prized musicianship of the more vigorous sort.

Williams began learning to play the piano as a toddler, and by her early teens she was playing in a vaudeville band. By 1930, she had joined the Clouds of Joy Orchestra, whose advertising billed her as "The Lady Who Swings the Band." Her scores, such as "Walkin' and Swingin'" and "Froggy Bottom," made Clouds of Joy one of the most popular swing bands of the 1930s, and led to requests for her arrangements from the likes of Louis Armstrong.

In 1942, Williams settled in New York, where she became a proponent of jazz's bebop revolution. At the same time, she expanded her range in yet another direction, with the composition of *Zodiac Suite*. It consisted of twelve symphonic jazz pieces, each evoking a certain musician, from Claude Debussy to Duke Ellington. In her later composing, Williams turned to religious themes, and among her most notable works was "Mary Lou's Mass," which became the score for a ballet choreographed by Alvin Ailey in 1971.

The jam session where this picture was shot included many of the jazz greats of the time and was, according to photographer Gjon Mili, "a spectacle *non pareil.*"

# Mary Lou Williams
1910–1981
*Jazz pianist, composer, arranger*

GJON MILI
(1904–1984)
Gelatin silver print
33.9 × 26.7 cm (13⅜ × 10½ in.)
1943

Hannah Arendt and her portrait photographer, Fred Stein, had much in common. Both of German-Jewish origin, they had fled Germany shortly after the rise of Adolf Hitler in 1933. Well educated—he as a lawyer and she with a doctorate in philosophy—they had both originally sought refuge in Paris and ultimately settled in New York City. And the upheavals in their lives had prevented them both from pursuing their intended career paths. When Stein shot this likeness in 1944, the trained jurist had long since become a photographer, and Arendt, once headed for a professor's chair, was a freelance journalist and research director for the Conference on Jewish Relations.

Arendt, however, had not divorced herself entirely from her academic past. By the late 1940s, she was at work on a volume probing into the cultural and political conditions that had led to Hitler's dictatorship and the absolutism of the Soviet Union's Joseph Stalin. Titled *The Origins of Totalitarianism,* the book created a sensation on its publication in 1951 and earned Arendt a reputation as a political theorist and historian to be reckoned with.

In the wake of *Origins,* Arendt became a much sought-after guest lecturer. Meanwhile, she continued to write, and in 1958, she published *The Human Condition,* in which she examined modern-day society's indifference to the life of the mind. On the publication of a collection of her essays, *Between Past and Future,* three years later, one admirer numbered Arendt among "the most brilliant … of living political philosophers."

One of Arendt's most endearing traits was her very genuine delight in the free interchange of ideas. Her publisher once confessed to her that he had borrowed some of her work for something he had written, without acknowledging the source. "Isn't that marvelous! That's what it's for," she replied.

# Hannah Arendt
## 1906–1975
### *Political philosopher*

FRED STEIN
(1909–1967)
Gelatin silver print
35 × 27.7 cm (13⅞ × 10⅞ in.)
1944 (printed 1987)
Gift of Peter Stein

Photographer Philippe Halsman depicted Marian Anderson in the manner that she most wanted to be remembered—as a singer in the act of performing. But by the time the picture was taken in 1945, Anderson was more than just a widely acclaimed singer. Ever since 1939, when she sang at the Lincoln Memorial after being barred on racial grounds from performing at Constitution Hall in Washington, D.C., she had also been a potent symbol of the drive for racial equality.

In Anderson's mid-teens, the Philadelphia church in whose choir she sang thought well enough of her gifts to raise funds for voice lessons. In the prevailing racial climate, however, her subsequent attempts to perform on the American concert circuit met with little success. As a result, she spent much of the early 1930s performing in Europe, where audiences were immediately enchanted by her rich contralto voice. In Salzburg, conductor Arturo Toscanini told her, "A voice like yours is heard once in a hundred years."

In the face of such praise, Anderson's own country could overlook her no longer. Returning to the United States in 1935, she gave her first concert at New York City's Town Hall, where she was proclaimed "mistress of all she surveyed."

For years, racism kept Anderson from performing with any major opera company. Finally, in 1955, the Metropolitan Opera invited her to sing in Verdi's *Un ballo in maschera*. Anderson's voice was past its peak. Still, the audience was enraptured, and when she took her curtain calls, many wept. The object of that emotional display had always shied from civil rights agitation, saying she was not "designed for hand to hand combat." Nevertheless, she had poked openings in America's racial barriers that most activists had only dreamed about.

# Marian Anderson
## 1897–1993
### *Singer*

PHILIPPE HALSMAN
(1906–1979)
Gelatin silver print
34.7 × 27.3 cm (13 ¹¹/₁₆ × 10¾ in.)
1945
Gift of George R. Rinhart

orn into a family known for its princely wealth, Peggy Guggenheim grew up in luxury, but inherited only a modest fortune thanks to her father's misinvestments. Still, it was enough to finance an unfocused bohemian life in Europe, consorting with the avant garde and taking a succession of lovers. As one observer put it, Guggenheim was "a member not of the Lost, but of the Mislaid Generation."

But by her late thirties, Guggenheim was bored, and in her search for something to do, she settled on opening a gallery in London specializing in modernism. The venture lost money, but Guggenheim decided that as long as she was at it, she might "just as well lose a lot more" by assembling a collection of modern art and creating a museum for it. Soon she was snapping up modernist works all over Europe. In late 1942, having shifted her venue from London to New York, Guggenheim opened Art of This Century, a combination museum and commercial gallery on West 57th Street. The conventionally minded did not know what to make of this vast array of modernism, but for Manhattan's more adventurous gallerygoers it soon became a "must-see."

Art of This Century lasted only until 1947, when Guggenheim moved to Venice. But in its brief existence, Guggenheim exercised a considerable impact in promoting the cause of modernism and in winning acceptance for such avant-garde American artists as Jackson Pollock and Mark Rothko.

In this photograph, Guggenheim sits looking toward a concave mirror in her New York apartment. On the closet doors hang an assortment of the showy earrings that she collected in great quantity and often used as wall decorations. Echoing the picture's surreal feel is the painting behind Guggenheim, *The Break of Day* by Belgian Surrealist Paul Delvaux.

# Peggy Guggenheim
1898–1979
*Art dealer, patron*

ANDRÉ KERTÉSZ
(1894–1985)
Gelatin silver print
34.8 × 27.8 cm (13¹¹⁄₁₆ × 10¹⁵⁄₁₆ in.)
1945

The future Gypsy Rose Lee began life as Rose Louise Hovick, the daughter of a ruthless stage mother who had her performing with her younger sister June on the vaudeville circuit by the time she was seven. With June as the star and Rose in the background chorus, the act did quite well for a while. But after June's elopement forced Rose into the star position, its bookings declined. Finally, in desperation, the act began taking engagements at burlesque houses, and it was in one of these less reputable venues that Rose Louise, at age fifteen, agreed one night to fill in for one of the show's stripteasers. So began Rose Louise Hovick's transformation into Gypsy Rose Lee, America's most famous practitioner of the art of disrobing.

One secret of Lee's success was a coy sophistication that often withheld from audiences some of what they expected without making them feel cheated. As Lee herself once explained, "You don't have to be naked to look naked. You just have to think naked." Armed with that outlook, she soon eclipsed her more blatantly suggestive competitors. According to Billy Minsky, proprietor of the leading New York burlesque house, she purged the striptease of its bump-and-grind crudities and turned it into "seven minutes of sheer art." Moreover, the intelligent wit evidenced in her performances eventually won her a respectability enjoyed by no other stripper. Pundit H.L. Mencken, feeling that what Lee did on stage merited the coinage of a new word, declared her an "ecdysiast," a term derived from two Greek words meaning "to get out" and "to molt."

The setting for Lee's portrait reflects her avid interest in collecting art and antiques. But the picture also evokes a strong sense of the "queenly style" that contributed to her uniqueness.

# Gypsy Rose Lee
## 1911–1970
*Entertainer*

ARNOLD NEWMAN
(1918–2006)
Gelatin silver print
24.8 × 32.9 cm (9¾ × 12¹⁵⁄₁₆ in.)
1945 (printed later)

Athlete Babe Didrikson Zaharias could be irritatingly loud, and her boasts to competitors like *"I'm* the star and all of you are the chorus" put her out of the running in any congeniality contest. But Didrikson had one undeniable virtue: She *was* indeed the star she claimed to be.

Not only that, Didrikson was a star at just about any sport she tried. In swimming, she missed setting a hundred-yard freestyle record by one second. She once threw a football 47 yards (43 m). In 1932, at the Amateur Athletic Union women's track and field championships, she won firsts in five events, and at the summer Olympics that year, she claimed gold medals in both the eighty-meter hurdles and the javelin throw.

But the sport in which Didrikson made her most lasting mark was golf. Not long after taking her first golf lesson in 1933, she qualified for tournament competition, and in 1935, she took the Texas Amateur Championship, the first of forty amateur titles she would ultimately win. Commenting on her incredible skill as she won the British Ladies' Amateur Championship in 1947, a spectator whispered, "She must be Superman's sister." But Didrikson explained her success on that occasion in an earthier manner. "I just loosen my girdle," she said, "and let the ball have it."

A founder of the Ladies Professional Golf Association in 1948, Didrikson proved to be the LPGA's biggest draw and most frequent purse-winner. By the time she died of cancer in 1956, she had claimed thirty-one LPGA titles.

This photograph was part of a series of shots that appeared in the Sunday Coloroto section of the *New York Daily News* on October 12, 1947. The object of the pictures was to show the form that had made Didrikson "Queen of the Links."

Mildred "Babe"
Didrikson Zaharias
1911–1956
*Athlete*

HARRY WARNECKE
(1900–1984)
and Robert Cranston (active circa 1937–1949)
Color carbro print
41.4 × 31.4 cm (16⅕₁₆ × 12⅜ in.)
1947

WARNECKE

Lillian Hellman had no idea what she wanted to do when she dropped out of Columbia in 1924, but a serendipitous connection at a party landed her a job as a publisher's manuscript reader. By 1930, she was a script reader in Hollywood and beginning an affair with mystery writer Dashiell Hammett.

Hellman now harbored ambitions to write drama, and it was Hammett who suggested patterning her first dramatic plot on the true story of two Scottish women whose lives were ruined by false allegations of lesbian behavior. The suggestion was a godsend. In that dark tale, Hellman found the framework for *The Children's Hour*, which, when it opened on Broadway in 1934, established her as a playwright of great promise.

Hellman's next play, *The Little Foxes*, met with yet greater acclaim at its New York opening in 1939. Unlike so many plays, which become dated after a few years, this grim drama of intrafamily greed won a critical respect that has proved enduring. Writer John Malcolm Brinnin once noted that with each reading of it, his admiration only increased. "It was like a Chinese box," he said, "each piece fitting precisely with the next."

Hellman returned to her characters in *The Little Foxes* to create *Another Part of the Forest*, staged in 1946. The play's success was probably what prompted *Vogue* to commission photographer Irving Penn to make this portrait of Hellman. Never published by the magazine, the likeness evokes the solid and unsentimental intelligence that went into the creation of her plays. But there was a softer side to Hellman, particularly when it came to the opposite sex. "Put a good-looking man in front of her," a female friend once said, and the southern-bred Hellman "became … Miss Lilly of New Orleans."

# Lillian Hellman
1905?–1984
*Writer*

IRVING PENN
(born 1917)
Gelatin silver print
17.9 × 19.2 cm (7 $\frac{1}{16}$ × 7 $\frac{9}{16}$ in.)
1947

Singer Billie Holiday did not have a big voice, and her range did not extend beyond an octave. Nevertheless, she was, by almost universal agreement, "the greatest female jazz voice of all time." She turned even the most unremarkable of pop songs into "iridescent gems," and her impact on other singers was incalculable. According to Frank Sinatra, almost "every major pop singer … [of] her generation" was "touched … by her genius."

Holiday got her first taste of jazz from the records that she heard as she did chores at a bordello in her native Baltimore. But this early exposure planted no thoughts of being a singer, and when she ventured into the entertainment world in the early 1930s, she was hoping to become a dancer in a New York speakeasy. At one tryout that went especially poorly, however, she was asked to sing, and her auditors were sufficiently impressed to hire her as a late-shift vocalist.

As Holiday developed her soft, intimate style and perfected her ability to improvise, she gradually built a following, and by the late 1930s, she was performing with the big-league bands of Count Basie and Artie Shaw. In about 1941, however, she became addicted to heroin, and her addiction soon began taking its toll on her performance. By the 1950s, her voice had lost much of its wonderful elasticity.

This image is thought to date from 1948, not long after Holiday had finished serving a jail sentence for possession of drugs. At her first post-incarceration concert, held at Carnegie Hall, the crowd greeted her performance with "hysterical applause." Alluding to her drug problems shortly thereafter, she said, "That's all over now; this is a new life." Unfortunately, that was not the case. Early the next year, she was again arrested for drug possession.

# Billie Holiday
1915–1959
*Singer*

SID GROSSMAN
(1913–1955)
Gelatin silver print
33.5 × 27.2 cm (13³⁄₁₆ × 10¹¹⁄₁₆ in.)
circa 1948

By her early twenties, Georgia O'Keeffe did not see much point in pursuing her painting ambitions if it meant simply following the conservative representational paths that her artistic training had fostered. "I began to realize," she recalled years later, "that a lot of people had done this same kind of painting … and I didn't think I could do it any better." So ruminating, she was soon charting a new way for herself.

Inspired by the modernist urgings of artist-theorist Arthur Wesley Dow simply "to fill space in a beautiful way," O'Keeffe began a series of charcoal abstractions in 1915 that sought to do just that. Eventually these works found their way to photographer Alfred Stieglitz's 291 gallery in New York, which was the hub of modernism in American art. Stieglitz, who would marry O'Keeffe in 1924, was so impressed that he soon featured the drawings in an exhibition without even asking her.

Best known for her austere, magnified renderings of flowers and her crisp depictions of the arid New Mexico landscape, O'Keeffe never entirely rejected realism. Instead, she gave it an abstractionist edge. For those who liked to fit artists into categories, this sometimes posed a problem. But regardless of where O'Keeffe fitted, there was little doubt of her stature. By the late 1930s, she numbered among America's most respected painters.

O'Keeffe had a striking appearance that echoed the austere character of her pictures. Even in this photograph, where there is clearly no attempt to flatter, she retains her arresting dignity and brings to mind the admirer who once described her as "the unflickering flame of a candle, steady, serene, softly brilliant."

# Georgia O'Keeffe
## 1887–1986
### Artist

IRVING PENN
(born 1917)
Platinum-palladium print
58.1 × 44 cm (22⅞ × 17⁵⁄₁₆ in.)
1948 (printed 1986)
Gift of Irving Penn

When Helena Rubinstein arrived from her native Poland in Australia, where she had gone to live on her uncle's sheep ranch, tucked into her luggage were pots of facial cream concocted by a Hungarian doctor. In a country where the pounding sun took a dreadful toll on female complexions, the cream's tonic effect on Rubinstein's skin drew envious compliments that suggested, in turn, an unusually splendid commercial opportunity. By 1902, Rubinstein was selling her Hungarian cream in a Melbourne shop. By 1915, she had parlayed that enterprise into a string of thriving beauty spas in London, Paris, and New York City, and within another decade the success of her spas and cosmetic lines had made her the world's best-known businesswoman.

"It doesn't matter how shaky a woman's hand is. She can still apply makeup," Rubinstein once observed, and that enduring impulse to improve on nature was certainly a significant factor in the creation of her fortune. But Rubinstein's own drive was more crucial yet. A relentless bargainer, she could be quite demanding of her employees and imperiously unpleasant when they displeased her. She was most demanding of herself, however, and her preoccupation with business remained unrelenting, so much so that she could not be bothered with the skin-care rituals that she urged on other women. "I tell you I am a worker," she once explained. "I have no time for it."

This image was taken for an article on Rubinstein in *Collier's* magazine, which billed her as "a John D. Rockefeller in petticoated miniature." The portrait did not run with the piece, but whatever the reason for not using it, it had nothing to do with the image's weak impact. Her hand placed firmly on her hip, the four-foot, ten-inch Rubinstein leaves no doubt here about who is in charge.

# Helena Rubinstein
1870–1965
*Businesswoman*

ARNOLD NEWMAN
(1918–2006)
Gelatin silver print
32.4 × 25.9 cm (12 ¾ × 10 ³/₁₆ in.)
1948 (printed later)
Gift of Arnold Newman

Anthropologist Margaret Mead was the author of more than thirty books and scores of articles. She also found room in her life to teach, work as a curator of anthropology at New York City's American Museum of Natural History, and travel the lecture circuit. Over time, her areas of expertise ranged ever more widely—from child-rearing practices in less developed societies to national character to ecology and culture-related problems of nutrition. Of her nonstop expansion of interests and crowded schedule she once said, "I expect to die but don't plan to retire."

In 1925, having completed her doctorate in anthropology at Columbia University, Mead went to American Samoa to study adolescence in the island's native culture. When her research reached book form as *Coming of Age in Samoa* in 1928, it enjoyed the best of all possible worlds. While drawing much praise from her profession, it also appealed to the general public, and it is still considered a pathbreaking work today.

In *Coming of Age*, Mead's findings supported the relatively new notion that many behavior patterns once thought to be mostly predetermined by biological inheritance resulted largely from cultural conditioning. In *Sex and Temperament in Three Primitive Societies*, published in 1935, Mead explored that hypothesis further, offering convincing evidence that cultural influences shaped gender roles far more than many behavior experts had hitherto acknowledged.

Mead sat for this photograph in the late 1940s, about the time she was bringing out *Male and Female: A Study of the Sexes in a Changing World.* In an interview coinciding with the book's publication in 1949, the interviewer described Mead as "a friendly but determined-looking woman" who did not overweight her conversation with the "technical terms" of her profession.

# Margaret Mead
1901–1978
*Anthropologist*

LOTTE JACOBI
(1896–1990)
Gelatin silver print
17.2 × 18.2 cm (6¾ × 7³⁄₁₆ in.)
1949

For most of Anna Robertson Moses's life, farmwork had been the central fact of her existence. But when farming became too much for her in her late seventies, she had to find other ways to fill her time. After arthritis made embroidery too painful, she discovered that her hand felt fine wielding a paintbrush, and in 1938, using paint and thresher cloth found in a barn, she created her first painting. Before long, she was passing the time producing scenes recalling the rural past of her younger days. When a New York City art collector spotted four of her paintings in 1939 in a drugstore in Hoosick Falls, New York, he was immediately charmed by their flat, untutored simplicity. After snapping up the four pictures, he went out to Moses's farm nearby and purchased all the pictures she had on hand.

By late the next year, newspaper critics were calling her "Grandma" Moses, and her work was being featured in a Manhattan gallery. At age eighty, the self-taught Moses had indeed arrived. Over the next twenty years, her idyllic renderings of farm life would become icons of the way Americans liked to remember their rural heritage. "Most of us would be bored to death" in the world that her pictures recalled, one critic admitted. But as presented by Moses, it all seemed utterly entrancing.

Taken in Grandma Moses's Eagle Bridge farmhouse, this portrait dates from 1949, the same year Moses went to Washington, D.C., to receive an achievement award from the Women's National Press Club. Stopping in New York City on her way to the nation's capital, she told reporters, "It's nice to be here, but the city doesn't appeal to me." "As picture material?" someone asked. "As any material," she answered.

# Anna Mary Robertson ("Grandma") Moses
## 1860–1961
*Artist*

ARNOLD NEWMAN
(1918–2006)
Gelatin silver print
45.9 × 36.9 cm (18$^1/_{16}$ × 14$^1/_2$ in.)
1949 (printed later)

At about the time this picture was taken, *Time* magazine noted that its subject, Eleanor Roosevelt, had "reversed the usual lot of presidents' widows." Instead of retreating into obscurity following Franklin Roosevelt's death in 1945, she had "become, perhaps, the best known woman in the world" and the "most popular living American" to boot.

Roosevelt's reputation could be attributed in part to the great residue of admiration that had accrued to her during her twelve-year tenure as first lady. Visibly involved in her husband's New Deal administration, she often acted as its moral conscience, and during World War II, she became one of the country's most effective and tireless morale builders as she visited Allied nations and comforted wounded soldiers in military hospitals. For a wartime goodwill ambassador, it was widely agreed that Franklin Roosevelt "could have made no better selection."

But even when FDR was still alive, Eleanor Roosevelt's stature was less and less defined by identification with her husband's presidency, and after his death she went on to perhaps her most enduring achievement, as a delegate to the newly formed United Nations. In 1946, she became chairman of the UN's Preliminary Commission on Human Rights (made permanent a year later) and presided over the drafting of the Universal Declaration of Human Rights. In doing so, she found herself traversing a hazardous terrain of clashing cultural ideals and national agendas. Armed with an endless supply of patient tact and a sunny candor that could be disarmingly childlike, she eluded its pitfalls successfully. When the UN's General Assembly endorsed the declaration in late 1948, no one deserved more credit than Roosevelt. Speaking of her role, one colleague claimed that he had never seen "naïveté and cunning so gracefully blended."

# Eleanor Roosevelt
1884–1962
*First lady, humanitarian*

CLARA E. SIPPRELL
(1885–1975)
Gelatin silver print
22.6 × 17.6 cm (8⅞ × 6¹³⁄₁₆ in.)
1949
Bequest of Phyllis Fenner

This photograph has a sense of cathartic letdown about it, but in this case it was letdown of the sweetest sort. The time of the picture's taking was the wee morning hours of January 6, 1950, and the trio seated on the sofa were (left to right) singer-actress Ethel Waters, writer Carson McCullers, and actress Julie Harris. Earlier that evening, Waters and Harris had opened on Broadway in McCullers's stage adaptation of her novel *The Member of the Wedding*, and the post-opening party was drawing to a close. But preceding the inertial quiet recorded here, a goodly amount of jubilant celebration had prevailed, for the evening had been an unalloyed triumph for all three women.

In summing up McCullers's success in transforming her novel into a drama, *New York Times* critic Brooks Atkinson had used terms like "masterly" and "wonderfully, almost painfully, perceptive." As for Ethel Waters's portrayal of Berenice the cook, Atkinson had described it as "rich and eloquent."

But perhaps the member of this trio who had experienced the greatest elation on this opening night was Julie Harris. Unlike McCullers and Waters, who had won plaudits before, the twenty-four-year-old Harris had been working in largely unappreciated anonymity until this time. Obscurity, however, ceased to be her lot in the wake of her perfectly pitched depiction of the play's motherless twelve-year-old tomboy. Harris had not fully registered what was happening to her as scores of well-wishers toasted her with champagne in her dressing room. But as the rave reviews began coming in several hours later, even she understood: There was now "a new star in the theater," and her name was Julie Harris.

Ethel Waters (1896–1977) *Singer, actress*
Carson McCullers (1917–1967) *Writer*
Julie Harris (born 1925) *Actress*

RUTH ORKIN
(1921–1985)
Gelatin silver print
18.3 × 23.9 cm (7⁹⁄₁₆ × 9⁷⁄₁₆ in.)
1950

This photograph of 1952 should perhaps be titled "the last leaf on the tree," which is how its subject, Frances Perkins, described herself not long after it was taken. Perkins had come to Washington, D.C., in March 1933 as secretary of labor in Franklin Roosevelt's New Deal administration, and she was soon part of the New Deal's unprecedented efforts to relieve the nation's economic depression and redefine the role of government in American life. Now, having headed the Department of Labor until 1945 and served some seven years on the Civil Service Commission, Perkins was retiring, and as she was the only major New Deal figure still in federal harness, "last leaf" was an apt metaphor indeed.

A pioneering promoter of worker welfare in New York State for more than two decades, Perkins was well qualified to be a secretary of labor. Nevertheless, this first woman ever to hold a cabinet post never managed to win more than grudging acceptance in many quarters. United Mine Workers head John L. Lewis called her "woozy in the head," and one observer characterized the welcome she often received from both labor and management as no more than "grim, polite, and unimpressed."

Behind many of the attacks on Perkins was the fact that she was a woman in what was deemed to be strictly a man's job. On that point, she once conceded, "The accusation that I am a woman is incontrovertible." But ultimately the best ripostes to critics lay in her accomplishments, which included primary roles in shaping such measures as the National Labor Relations Act and the Social Security Act. In 1944, a columnist who generally had nothing good to say about FDR's New Deal opined that "the argument can be made that Miss Perkins is the best" secretary of labor ever.

# Frances Perkins
1880–1965
*Cabinet official*

CLARA E. SIPPRELL
(1885–1975)
Gelatin silver print
25.2 × 20.3 cm (9¹⁵/₁₆ × 8 in.)
1952

"Here is a remarkable artist who ... will rank among the great dancers of her time," wrote *New York Times* critic John Martin after seeing Carmelita Maracci perform in 1937. In a program showcasing Maracci's original blend of classical ballet and Spanish dance, Martin noted that she had done one number "seated throughout on an old-fashioned circular piano stool." The mere idea of trying such a thing, he admitted, sounded "slightly ludicrous." But when Maracci did it, he said that she became "an abstract of Spain in the dance, a projection of the spirit of the dance."

Despite her genius, Maracci never achieved the broad recognition that she deserved. At the heart of the problem was a high-strung temperament that made for unreliability. Her violent reaction to a drunk in the audience at one of her concerts in 1946 forced the cancellation of the rest of her tour. Five years later, when the first of several appearances at the Ballet Theatre in New York did not go as well as she had hoped, she called off the rest of her performances. On another occasion, she backed out of starring in *Giselle* after a few rehearsals because the role made her feel imbecilic.

Although her fame as a performer was never widespread, Maracci had considerable impact as a teacher. Among her students were any number of distinguished dance figures, including Jerome Robbins and Cynthia Gregory, and many of them considered her to be a primary mentor.

This picture appears to have caught Maracci in one of her frequent solitary practice sessions. The picture's maker, Bob Willoughby, was just the photographer to record such a moment. As a Hollywood freelancer, he specialized in capturing performers in the more private milieu of rehearsal and preparation.

# Carmelita Maracci
## 1911–1987
*Dancer*

BOB WILLOUGHBY
(born 1927)
Gelatin silver print
25.2 × 26.4 cm (9¹⁵/₁₆ × 10⅜ in.)
1953 (printed 1991)
Gift of Mr. and Mrs. Bob Willoughby

"I never knew anyone with a passion for words who had as much difficulty in saying things as I do," poet Marianne Moore once said. "Help is needed: you need a horse, a boat, to help you." With the works in her *Complete Poems* (published in 1967) numbering only 120, she was obviously stating the truth. But the end result was well worth the agony. In 1941, critic Malcolm Cowley ranked the title poem of her volume *What Are Years* "among the noblest lyrics of our time." Ten years later, Moore was hailed as "just about the most accomplished poetess alive." Along with such praise came nearly every important award a poet could win, including a Pulitzer Prize, the Bollingen Prize in Poetry, and a National Book Award.

Moore's poems were often difficult to penetrate, but she saw nothing wrong in that, claiming "it ought to be work to read something that was work to write." It meant, however, that her audience remained relatively small. But in an homage to her beloved Brooklyn Dodgers, entitled "Hometown Piece for Messrs. Alston and Reese," she struck a chord that could be readily appreciated by many. "As for Gil Hodges, in custody of first—," ran one of its passages, "'He'll do it by himself.' Now a specialist—versed / in an extension reach far into the box seats— / he lengthens up, leans and gloves the ball."

Moore's poems were filled with animal imagery, and when *Life* did a story on her in 1953, it featured pictures of her at the Bronx Zoo captioned with passages from her poems. The one for this image came from "Elephants" and ended with "these knowers 'arouse the feeling that they are / allied to man' and can change roles with their trustees."

# Marianne Moore
1887–1972
*Poet*

ESTHER BUBLEY
(1921–1998)
Gelatin silver print
24.9 × 34 cm (9¹³⁄₁₆ × 13⅝ in.)
1953

Although the details of the story vary in the telling, it is clear that Ella Fitzgerald's performing career began in the mid-1930s, at an amateur talent show in Harlem. She had entered the show on a dare, and her intention was to perform a dance. But once on stage, she froze up, and the best she could do was to get out a rendition of the popular song "The Object of My Affection." This fallback alternative, however, proved good enough to win the contest, and so began Fitzgerald's rise as one of America's most admired popular vocalists. By the close of the 1930s, she would be "The First Lady of Swing."

Part of Fitzgerald's charm was her unprepossessing manner, which made audiences warm to her immediately. But the main attraction was a silver-smooth voice that could span three octaves with seamless ease. That suppleness was tailor-made for the improvisational flights that she began perfecting in the 1940s, which would earn her still another title, "Queen of Scat."

Yet another Fitzgerald asset was her intuitive understanding of a song composer's intentions and her willingness to honor them. Rather than "renovate" a song according to her taste, she "came to inhabit" it, and among her warmest fans were composers. "I never knew how good our songs were," lyricist Ira Gershwin once said, "until I heard Ella Fitzgerald sing them."

This image of Fitzgerald is thought to have been taken in 1954, the year she performed at the first Newport Jazz Festival. According to someone who saw her there, she was nervous about how other musicians would judge her performance. She need not have worried. She soon had the crowd "in a frenzy," and when she was done, "the roar was deafening."

# Ella Fitzgerald
1917–1996
*Singer*

LISETTE MODEL
(1901–1983)
Gelatin silver print
34.9 × 27.5 cm (13¾ × 10¹⁵/₁₆ in.)
circa 1954

Taken during the filming of *A Star Is Born*, this photograph captures singer-actress Judy Garland at both her epic worst and her epic best.

One of the great adolescent stars of the second half of the 1930s, she had won the adoration of young and old alike as Dorothy in *The Wizard of Oz* in 1939, and her teaming with Mickey Rooney in the Andy Hardy films had been a box-office favorite. By this time, however, her difficult temperament and drug problems had made her "the star of her own adult melodrama."

As played out on the set of *A Star Is Born*, the melodrama expressed itself in outbursts of temper and failures to show up for shootings. Eventually this behavior drove the movie's costs to more than five million dollars, making it Hollywood's second most expensive film up to that time. At one point, the exasperated director, George Cukor, confided to Katharine Hepburn that Garland was definitely "unhinged."

The one thing that was not unhinged, however, was Garland's showmanship. In that department, she managed to turn in a spectacular performance, which, according to one critic, made *A Star Is Born* "just about the greatest one-woman show in modern movie history."

Unfortunately, this success was not exactly a harbinger of better things to come, and the remaining fifteen years of Garland's life were fraught with personal unhappiness and health problems. Nevertheless, her passion for performing remained strong and led to a number of concerts in which she mesmerized fans with her songs and dancing. One of the most memorable of those appearances took place at New York City's Carnegie Hall in 1961. Even a critic who was not much of a Garland fan had to admit that he left the hall "knowing that he had heard the best belter in the business."

# Judy Garland
1922–1969
*Singer, actress*

BOB WILLOUGHBY
(born 1927)
Gelatin silver print
35.2 × 21.4 cm (13¹⁵/₁₆ × 8⅜ in.)
1954 (printed 1977)
Gift of Mr. and Mrs. Bob Willoughby

Few people contemplating Marilyn Monroe in early 1954 would have doubted that she was a Hollywood star of the first magnitude. In the previous year, her films *Gentlemen Prefer Blondes* and *How to Marry a Millionaire* had been box-office smashes. But more important, with a figure approaching perfection and a face to match, she was undoubtedly the most celebrated sex symbol ever to come out of Hollywood.

One person, however, remained skeptical of Monroe's stardom, and that was Monroe herself, whose deep-seated insecurities still made her unsure of her own success. But even she became a believer in February 1954, as she entertained American troops in Korea. Poured into a low-cut sheath, she was a sensation as she cooed and sang before thousands of GIs. The soldiers could not get enough of it. And neither could Monroe, who said that her Korean shows had been "the best thing that ever happened to me." "I never felt like a star before in my heart," she told a friend. "It was so wonderful to look down and see a fellow smiling at me."

More precisely, it was fellows—acres of them, gaping, cheering, and snapping pictures. Among them was Navy Hospitalman Second Class David Geary, who, in a case of mistaken identity, found himself in the front rows reserved for officers. It was from that privileged position that he took this picture.

Unfortunately, the euphoria that Monroe felt as Geary clicked his camera was by no means permanent, and her constant insecurity would always make it excruciatingly difficult for anyone to work with her. Even so, no one would deny her screen impact. As director Billy Wilder put it, after her death in 1962, capturing "three luminous minutes" of Monroe was eminently worth the "week's torment" that it sometimes took to get them.

# Marilyn Monroe
1926–1962
*Actress*

DAVID D. GEARY
(1930–1999)
Silver dye bleach print
23.5 × 34.8 cm (9¼ × 13¹¹/₁₆ in.)
1954 (printed 1998)
Gift of David D. Geary

In late 1932, Dorothy Day went to Washington, D.C., to write an article for *Commonweal* on a Communist-sponsored hunger march. Had she still been the radical idealist of her youth, she might have joined the demonstration. By this time, however, she no longer felt much affinity for its extremist organizers. Instead, having converted to Catholicism, she was seeking to vent her reformer's impulse in ways that were more in keeping with her religion. So, after observing the march, she went to the Shrine of the Immaculate Conception to pray for guidance.

The answer to Day's prayer came the next day, when a former Christian Brother named Peter Maurin visited her. Within a few months, the two had founded the *Catholic Worker*, a newspaper dedicated to redressing social injustices and promoting communal Christian values. As the newspaper's circulation quickly soared, its headquarters on New York's Lower East Side became a model for cooperative activism. By the mid-1930s, its premises were as much a soup kitchen and homeless shelter as they were editorial offices, and soon similar Catholic Worker "Houses of Hospitality" were springing up in cities across the United States.

Day's pacifism eroded support for the Catholic Worker Movement during World War II. But somehow the movement survived. At her funeral in 1980, anti-Vietnam activist Abbie Hoffman said Day was "the nearest this Jewish boy is ever going to get to a saint." It was just as well she could not hear that. "When they say you are a saint," she once mused, "what they mean is that you are not to be taken seriously."

This picture was taken for an article on Day in another Catholic publication, *Jubilee* magazine. Day was "quiet, even shy," noted the author of the piece, but when it came to defending the weak, she was "tirelessly outspoken."

# Dorothy Day
1897–1980
*Social activist, journalist*

VIVIAN CHERRY
(born 1920)
Gelatin silver print
16 × 23.7 cm (6⁵⁄₁₆ × 9⁵⁄₁₆ in.)
1955

W hen this picture was taken in the summer of 1955, no one would have suspected that its subject, Rosa Parks, would soon open a significant chapter in black civil rights militance. At that time, this long-time secretary of the Montgomery, Alabama, branch of the National Association for the Advancement of Colored People was attending a workshop in community activism at Highlander Folk School in Tennessee. But she doubted that she would be applying much of what she was learning at Highlander back in Montgomery, where even mild black agitation risked harsh reprisals.

Parks could not have been more wrong. On December 1, she was riding home on a bus from her job as a seamstress at a Montgomery department store. She was seated in the section reserved for blacks, but local regulations required that whenever the "whites only" section was filled, a black rider had to surrender his or her seat if a white person asked for it. When that situation arose on the bus that evening, however, Parks refused to stand up. Soon the police were called in, and she found herself under arrest.

Within hours, Parks's cause became the cause of Montgomery's entire black community, and the city's African American leadership was soon launching a boycott of the bus system to force integration in its seating and a concession to hire black drivers. As the boycott held, a case seeking to outlaw the bus system's segregationist practices moved through the courts. Finally, in December 1956, the boycott and the Supreme Court's decision banning Montgomery's bus segregation brought the struggle to a successful close. Parks's initial act of defiance had cost her her job. Nevertheless, she could find solace in the knowledge that she had sparked one of the great energizing events of the mid-twentieth century's civil rights movement.

# Rosa Parks
1913–2005
*Civil rights activist*

IDA BERMAN
(born 1911)
Gelatin silver print
25.1 × 19.5 cm (9⅞ × 7¹¹⁄₁₆ in.)
1955

In 1955, two years before she posed for this picture in New York City's Harlem, where she had grown up, Althea Gibson was feeling that the time had come for her to get out of competitive tennis. The sport had brought her a long way from her adolescent days as a streetwise tough and habitual school truant. In 1950, after claiming ten women's singles championships in competitions sponsored by the all-black American Tennis Association, she broke through the color barrier to become the first African American to compete for a title in the National Championship Tournament at Forest Hills. By 1953, she ranked seventh in American women's tennis. The next year, however, she dropped down to thirteen, and by late summer of 1955, she had decided to pursue a military career.

Before Gibson could do that, however, the State Department asked her to join a goodwill tennis tour in Southeast Asia, and she accepted. As the tour progressed, she encountered an acceptance that she had seldom felt in the overwhelmingly white world of American tennis, and suddenly her play soared to a new level. By the late spring of 1956, she was claiming the French Singles Championship, and the next year, she won the women's singles at Wimbledon and at the U.S. National competition at Forest Hills. As if that were not enough, she repeated that same pair of triumphs in 1958.

The lanky Gibson did not always look like the winner that she was. "Althea Gibson is not the most graceful figure on the courts," *Time* reported, "and her game is not the most stylish." Still, there was a power in her game that was unequaled, and according to a competitor, "she plays smarter all the time."

---

# Althea Gibson

1927–2003

*Athlete*

GENEVIEVE NAYLOR
(1915–1989)
Gelatin silver print
18.8 × 18.9 cm (7 3/8 × 7 7/16 in.)
1957 (printed circa 1970)

When this picture was taken, poet-novelist Sylvia Plath was living in Boston in the Beacon Hill apartment that she shared with her English poet husband, Ted Hughes. In many respects, this was probably the happiest period in Plath's adult life. She not only had a husband eminently sympathetic to her poetic ambitions, but also encouraging her was the older poet Robert Lowell, whose seminar she attended, as well as Anne Sexton, another young poet in the seminar, who became a close friend. With stimulation coming from all these quarters, Plath could feel her powers as a writer advancing steadily, and in May 1959, she wrote in her journal, "I have … overcome my fear of facing a blank page day after day, acknowledging myself, in my deepest emotions, a writer, come what may." By year's end, Plath had moved to England, and that optimism was finding the ultimate reinforcement as she prepared to bring out the first collection of her poetry, *The Colossus and Other Poems.*

Unfortunately, as evidenced by the turbulent despair expressed in her work, Plath was a fundamentally tormented individual, even at the best of times, and in early 1963 she committed suicide.

Within her own lifetime, Plath was never very widely known. Her later, posthumously published poems, however, indicate that her poetic gifts never stopped growing, and her importance in American poetry has long since been recognized. Adding further to her reputation is her novel, *The Bell Jar,* inspired by her student years at Smith College, which had been marked by both stellar achievement and emotional breakdown. In the early 1970s, this chronicle of a young woman trying to find herself in a world intent on stifling her individuality struck a meaningful chord among feminists, and made Plath a prophet of their cause.

# Sylvia Plath
1932–1963
*Poet, novelist*

ROLLIE McKENNA
(1918–2003)
Gelatin silver print
18.4 × 14 cm (7¼ × 5½ in.)
1959 (printed 1995)
Gift of Rollie McKenna

As a child, Lorraine Hansberry moved with her prosperous African American family into a white Chicago neighborhood that, like many urban residential enclaves of the time, had a covenant banning black residents. When the covenant was invoked to drive Hansberry's family from their new home, her father challenged its legality all the way to the Supreme Court, which declared it invalid in 1940. Unfortunately, the decision was unenforceable in the face of white Chicago's hostility to it, and Hansberry's father became convinced that fair treatment was something that blacks simply could never expect in the United States.

To say that those events left an impression on Hansberry is an understatement, and when she began crafting her play *A Raisin in the Sun* in 1956, she was to a large extent mining her own past as she built its plot around a black family's ambition to trade a ghetto apartment for a sunny house in a white neighborhood. Although many thought there was no audience for Hansberry's play, she finally found some willing backers, and in March 1959, *Raisin* opened on Broadway to a loud chorus of praise. Not long afterward, Hansberry became the first black playwright to win the New York Drama Critics Circle Award.

*A Raisin in the Sun* ended with the play's black family finally getting their house. Some playgoers interpreted that as a happy ending and faulted Hansberry for being a Pollyanna at a time when racism against African Americans continued to be such a great problem. Hansberry, however, knew full well that when *Raisin*'s black family moved into their house, their struggles against white bigotry had only just begun. Nowhere was that awareness more evident than in Hansberry's strong support in the early 1960s for the civil rights movement's ever-growing militance.

# Lorraine Hansberry
1930–1965
*Playwright*

DAVID MOSES ATTIE
(1920–1983)
Gelatin silver print
34.6 × 27.3 cm (13⅝ × 10¾ in.)
circa 1960

In the mid-1950s, Anne Sexton's repeated mental breakdowns sent her into therapy and, acting on the suggestion of her doctor, she began trying to understand her emotional difficulties by writing poetry. What began as a therapeutic exercise soon became a vocation, and as Sexton used her verse to probe the dark recesses of her mind, she aligned herself with the so-called "confessional" poets. With the publication in 1960 of the first collection of her work, *To Bedlam and Part Way Back*, she was recognized as an important new voice in American poetry.

Taken the following year, this photograph of Sexton seems to depict a woman at ease with herself and her newfound fame. She appears, in fact, to be one of those individuals who has the proverbial "all"—beauty and talent topped off by self-assurance. In 1961, that was indeed how she sometimes struck people. Meeting Sexton for the first time in April at the Cornell University Arts Festival, where she gave a reading, fellow poet Peter Davison thought that her pre-performance confession of anxiety was merely an act. Not only did she "read splendidly," but she also turned out to be a live wire afterward. "Once the parties started, she was going half the night," Davison recalled.

That was Sexton seen from the outside. From the inside, it was a different story. Reporting on the Cornell reading to her therapist, she said, "I was scared the whole time." Yet however intractable her emotional difficulties remained, Sexton's artistry thrived, and in 1967, her collection *Live or Die* earned a Pulitzer Prize. Unfortunately, neither accolades nor therapy could curb Sexton's vulnerability to recurring depression, and in 1974, she committed suicide.

# Anne Sexton
## 1928–1974
### *Poet*

ROLLIE McKENNA
(1918–2003)
Gelatin silver print
34.3 × 26.5 cm (13 1/2 × 10 7/16 in.)
1961 (printed 1995)
Gift of Rollie McKenna

There were many things that seemed to mark folk singer Joan Baez as singularly ill-cast for the role of a popular vocal artist. She suffered from severe shyness, which she made little effort to overcome, and she had rejected attempts to enhance her appeal through makeup or dress. When she came on stage, it was thus a rather stark affair—just a plainly clad, soft-spoken girl with a guitar. Nor was there a burning ambition driving Baez down her road to fame. After performing in coffeehouses around Boston for a few years, she went to the Newport Folk Festival in 1959 to perform, and was a great hit there. But when that success spawned recording offers and chances for concert tours, she turned them all down and went back to performing in Boston.

There was one plus, however, far outweighing the career-hampering minuses: Baez's soprano voice was an incredible instrument, "as lustrous and rich as old gold." Thanks to that voice, lack of showmanship mattered little when she finally began recording and doing tours. By mid-1962, Baez had sold more records than any other female folk singer in history, and her recent concert at Carnegie Hall had been sold out months in advance, despite little advertising.

This photograph was taken in 1963, during the great March on Washington to demand federal action guaranteeing equality for black Americans. At the Lincoln Memorial on August 28, the honor fell to Baez to lead the crowd in singing the civil rights movement's anthem, "We Shall Overcome." Recalling the scene years later, Baez noted that "one of the medals which hangs over my heart I awarded to myself for having been asked to sing that day."

# Joan Baez
born 1941
*Folk singer*

IVAN MASSAR
(born 1924)
Gelatin silver print
24.2 × 16.5 cm (9½ × 6½ in.)
1963

As photographer Bruce Davidson snapped this picture in Detroit's Motown recording studios in 1965, the three young women caught in his lens—from left to right, Florence Ballard, Diana Ross, and Mary Wilson—were rapidly scaling the heights of the pop music world. Originally calling themselves the Primettes, they had changed their name to the Supremes, and by 1965, they were indeed beginning to reign supreme. In the previous year, their single "Where Did Our Love Go" had reached number one on the hit charts, and its sales had topped two million. Over the next twelve months, five more of their songs climbed to number one, and by 1967, the Supremes were the most successful female group in pop history.

The key to the Supremes' success was without question lead singer Diana Ross, who had a voice that, as one critic said, could put "swerves into the most unsupple lyrics." But Ross also had a presence that was as riveting as her voice. With her lithe body "slung like six feet of limp wrist," one observer noted, "she stood under the velvet spotlight, a perfect summa-cum-laude Supreme."

Ross left the Supremes to strike out on her own in 1970. The move proved good for her, and she continued to enjoy immense popularity. For a reconstituted Supremes, however, the results were not nearly as positive. Although some of their recordings made the hit charts in the next several years, the group never again occupied the heights that it had with Ross.

Davidson's photograph of the Supremes was one of many that he shot of the group over several days in Detroit and New York City. As he worked around them, he said years later, they barely acknowledged him. Even so, he noted, "I enjoyed them as people, and they were gorgeous."

# Diana Ross born 1944
with fellow Supremes Florence Ballard and Mary Wilson
*Singers*

BRUCE DAVIDSON
(born 1933)
Gelatin silver print
20.4 × 35.3 cm (8 × 13⅞ in.)
1965

In August 1962, Fannie Lou Hamer walked into a civil rights meeting in Mississippi where the speakers were urging blacks to join in agitating for the rights so long denied them. Hamer got the message, and several days later she was challenging Mississippi's systematic disenfranchisement of blacks by trying to register to vote. After the effort failed, Hamer's employer threatened to fire her if she ever tried again. The intimidation did not work, however. The following January, she succeeded in registering and, in the process, found a new vocation for herself as a civil rights field worker.

Several months later, Hamer was brutally beaten in a Mississippi jail for venturing into a "whites only" lunchroom. But the experience only strengthened her commitment, and in 1964, she spearheaded a protest at the Democratic National Convention challenging the seating of Mississippi's delegation, which had been chosen under a system that excluded black participation. Hamer's group won a token compromise, which granted them two delegation seats, but she regarded this as a defeat. As she put it, "We didn't come all this way for no two seats when all of us is tired." Nevertheless, the war had been won. Hamer's compelling and nationally publicized convention testimony on Mississippi's methods for barring blacks from the political process had assured that the days of exclusionary politics in Mississippi and other southern states were numbered.

Fond of punctuating her public utterances with "I'm sick and tired of being sick and tired," Hamer went on in the late 1960s to found the Freedom Farm Cooperative, which ultimately provided food for some five thousand people. In the picture here, she is seen participating in the March Against Fear that James Meredith launched in June 1966 to dramatize the determination of southern blacks to gain their full measure of rights.

# Fannie Lou Hamer
## 1917–1977
### *Civil rights activist*

CHARMIAN READING
(born 1931)
Gelatin silver print
25.7 × 34 cm (10⅛ × 13⅜ in.)
1966 (printed later)

Not especially good-looking, somewhat overweight, and interested in painting and folk music, Janis Joplin fell well short of the image that might have won her a place among the cheerleading set in her native Port Arthur, Texas. As she summed it up years later, she was "just 'silly crazy Janis,'" the resident beatnik. After high school, Joplin's odd-man-out syndrome continued as she dropped in and out of college and took to singing in coffeehouses. But she finally found her niche in mid-1966, when she became the lead vocalist for Big Brother and the Holding Company, a San Francisco rock band organized by a Texas friend.

As Joplin reveled in San Francisco's vibrant hippie culture, her singing took on an uninhibited and shrilly aggressive exuberance that made her the city's hottest rock music attraction. Joplin ceased to be a mostly local phenomenon, however, in June 1967, when she electrified the Monterey International Pop Festival with her rendition of "Love Is Like a Ball and Chain." By the song's close, Joplin had become a major pop star. When it became known not long afterward that she and her group were coming out with their first album, *Cheap Thrills*, sales topped one million even before the record went on the market.

The feverish energy that Joplin poured into her performing, and her heavy drinking, prompted many to predict that she would quickly burn herself out. When asked about this, she said, "When I can't sing, I'll worry about it then." That was an eventuality, however, that she never faced. In October of 1970, Joplin was found dead from an overdose of heroin.

Taken several months after her Monterey performance, this picture depicts Joplin at New York City's Fillmore East, singing "Ball and Chain."

# Janis Joplin
1943–1970
*Singer*

LINDA McCARTNEY
(1942–1998)
Chromogenic print
50.7 × 40.5 cm (19 15/16 × 15 15/16 in.)
1967 (printed 1996)
Gift of the photographer,
Linda McCartney

From early on, Pauline Trigère was destined for a career in the clothing business. Raised in Paris, she was the daughter of a tailor and a seamstress. Even as a child, she knew how to get the most out of a bolt of cloth, and by her early twenties, she was married to a tailor. But although these factors portended a future in clothing manufacture, they could not anticipate that one day Trigère would be regarded as a leading designer in American fashion.

The ascent toward that eminence began with a French election in 1936 that put the socialists in power. Trigère's husband, fearing that this spelled the end of free enterprise in France, convinced his wife and her family to emigrate, and they eventually transplanted their clothing business to New York City. Unfortunately, both the business and Trigère's marriage failed, and by 1941, she was striking out on her own as a dressmaker. In quantity, her first collection of eleven dresses was not impressive, but their clean elegance certainly was. Before long, fashion buyers from the most prestigious stores were clamoring for her clothes. By 1949, she was claiming the Coty American Fashion Critics' Award.

On learning that a woman had been buried in a Trigère creation, the designer remarked, "You see? With a Trigère you can go anywhere!" Within that jest was a grain of seriousness that reflected Trigère's abiding concern for creating clothes with a versatility and elegance that made women feel good about wearing them for years.

Instead of drawing, Trigère designed by draping cloth on a live model, cutting and shaping it as she went. Described once as a "virtuoso with the shears," she rarely made an uncorrectable cut. "Put a piece of fabric in my hands," she once boasted, "and magic happens."

# Pauline Trigère
1909–2002
*Fashion designer*

ARTHUR LEIPZIG
(born 1918)
Gelatin silver print
22.8 × 34.2 cm (9 × 13⁷⁄₁₆ in.)
1968 (printed 1997)

In 1945, Diane Arbus and her husband, Alan, formed a partnership to do fashion photography for her family's women's store in New York City. The collaboration thrived, and their business gradually began to include commissions from leading fashion magazines. Arbus, however, came to feel deeply frustrated by the sameness of her work. Finally, her unhappiness reached a breaking point at a dinner party in 1957, where she broke into uncontrollable sobs when asked about her business. Shortly thereafter, she began exploring the possibilities of portraiture. But it was not portraiture shot in a studio. Rather, her likenesses were taken in venues that were part of her subjects' lives—their living rooms and neighborhood streets—and ultimately Arbus's images evolved into a distinctive meld of in situ spontaneity and photographer control.

The individuals in Arbus's photographs ranged from the famous to freakish eccentrics found on society's margins. But whether they documented the high or the low, her pictures tended to have one trait in common—an often adversarial candor that seemed to expose subjects at their most vulnerable point.

Not everyone appreciated that candor. One of Arbus's subjects, writer Norman Mailer, likened "giving a camera to Diane Arbus" to "putting a hand grenade in the hands of a child." On the other hand, the Museum of Modern Art curator John Szarkowski saw her candor as the reflection of a "truly generous spirit." By the time Arbus took her own life in 1971, a consensus was emerging that, likable or not, her pictures were the work of one of the most original practitioners of mid-twentieth-century photography.

The droll impact of Arbus's grim expression in this picture as she clenches a daffodil in her mouth calls to mind the remarkable stock of tricks she used to make subjects drop their defenses before her camera.

# Diane Arbus
## 1923–1971
*Photographer*

GARRY WINOGRAND
(1928–1984)
Gelatin silver print
31.2 × 47.1 cm (12 ⁹⁄₁₆ × 18 ⁹⁄₁₆ in.)
1969

Diana Vreeland grew up a daughter of privilege, and her pleasure-seeking parents never gave much thought to her formal schooling, which amounted to sporadic attendance at exclusive schools. Nevertheless, as Vreeland grew into young womanhood and married, she received an education that would prove quite valuable. Everywhere she turned in her upper-crust world there were lessons to learn in what was chic and stylish. Vreeland absorbed those lessons well, and when a drop in her husband's income forced her to take a job in the mid-1930s, she found a perfect match for her expertise: working at the fashion-minded *Harper's Bazaar*.

Vreeland's first work for the magazine was a frivolous column that offered readers such sophisticated counsels as "Why don't you … sweep into the drawing room … with an enormous red-fox muff of many skins?" But within a few years she had become *Harper's Bazaar*'s fashion editor, and by the time she became editor-in-chief at *Vogue* in the early 1960s, her influence in fashion was unrivaled. While designers "tremble[d] at her nod," many of their customers were inclined "to pick purely" on the basis of what she endorsed.

After leaving *Vogue* in 1971, Vreeland became a consultant for the Metropolitan Museum of Art's Costume Institute, and this picture was taken not long after the opening of her show for the museum on the clothing of Hollywood stars. The image underscores the irony that in a business where looks meant so much, Vreeland had herself been no great beauty. But the photograph also evokes a presence substantially greater than the sum of its parts. As one admirer put it, she was "a bird of paradise who took her plumage for granted," and when she walked into a room, even the more dazzling figures around her "melted into the background."

# Diana Vreeland
1903–1989
*Fashion editor*

ARNOLD NEWMAN
(1918–2006)
Gelatin silver print
33.1 × 25.1 cm (13 1/16 × 9 7/8 in.)
1974

After her husband's suicide in the summer of 1963, Katharine Graham had to decide whether she should try to succeed him as head of the family-owned media company and its flagship newspaper, the *Washington Post*. Although terrified at the prospect, she concluded that she had to try.

Recalling that decision years later, Graham said, "I … shut my eyes and step[ped] off the ledge. The surprise was that I landed on my feet." Actually, she did quite a bit more than that. Under her guidance, the *Washington Post* grew into one of the most influential newspapers in the world, and its parent company prospered mightily. As for Graham's personal reputation, by the mid-1970s she was being described as the "most powerful woman in journalism."

Among Graham's greatest strengths was her unswerving commitment to a free press. Even in the face of possible legal and economic reprisals, that commitment placed the *Post* in the vanguard in reporting the two most controversial news stories of the early 1970s—the airing of the Pentagon Papers relating to the Vietnam War, and the Watergate scandals that climaxed in Richard Nixon's presidential resignation.

Ever self-effacing about her accomplishments, Graham was not altogether confident that anyone would be much interested in the memoir she began writing in about 1990. The resulting book, however, proved a compelling exercise in candor and eventually won a Pulitzer Prize.

Graham's likeness was part of a portrait series of noted figures that photographer Richard Avedon took for *Rolling Stone* to mark America's bicentennial in 1976. While this starkly unadorned image may not be especially flattering, the picture suggests a stolidness that makes quite clear what prompted *Post* executive editor Ben Bradlee to describe Graham as someone with "the guts of a burglar."

# Katharine Graham
## 1917–2001
*Newspaper publisher, writer*

RICHARD AVEDON
(1923–2004)
Gelatin silver print
25.5 × 20.2 cm (10 ¹/₁₆ × 7 ¹⁵/₁₆ in.), 1976
This acquisition was made possible by generous contributions from Jeane W. Austin and the James Smithson Society

Photographer Richard Avedon's portraits sometimes seemed intended to erode their subjects' stature. But Texas Congresswoman Barbara Jordan filled the frame with a presence that seemed to dare Avedon to discover a weakness in her armor. Looking at this likeness, it is easy to understand why one journalist said that an interview with Jordan was "a bit like grilling God."

Jordan lived by the principle that she "never wanted to be run of the mill." As a young girl, she had decided against being a pharmacist because it was unlikely to lead to much distinction. Instead, she became a lawyer and then set her sights on winning public office. In 1966, she became the first woman elected to the Texas Senate and the first African American to sit in that body since the 1880s.

Elected to the U.S. House of Representatives in 1972, Jordan sat on its Judiciary Committee, which soon put her at the heart of the congressional investigation into whether President Richard Nixon's involvements in the Watergate scandals were grounds for impeachment. One commentator called Jordan "the best mind on the committee." But equally noteworthy was her gift for expressing herself, and her statement on July 24, 1974, recommending acceptance of the articles of impeachment against Nixon, was among the most memorable moments in Watergate rhetoric. No hyperbole, she said in her preamble, could "overstate the solemnness that I feel right now. My faith in the Constitution is whole. It is complete. It is total." Spoken by someone else, such declarations might have been dismissed as cynically calculated. But the carefully paced cadence of Jordan's delivery and the magisterial tone of her voice invested her words with a weight that seemed to strike exactly the right chord for this deeply troubling political occasion.

# Barbara Jordan
1936–1996
*Congresswoman, lawyer*

RICHARD AVEDON
(1923–2004)
Gelatin silver print
25.3 × 20.3 cm (9¹⁵⁄₁₆ × 8 in.), 1976
This acquisition was made possible by generous contributions from Jeane W. Austin and the James Smithson Society

Until well into her thirties, Julia Child never gave much thought to food. But when her husband's job took her to Paris in 1948, she began taking classes at France's world-famous Cordon Bleu cooking school. Within weeks her onetime indifference to culinary matters had been displaced by a nearly insatiable passion, and her husband was soon describing himself as the "Cordon Bleu widower."

Child's enthusiasm drew her into more ambitious enterprises. With two French friends, Simone Beck and Louisette Bertholle, she established a cooking school, which in turn led to a three-way collaboration on a French cookbook for the American market. The book's original intended publisher ultimately rejected it, thinking that it would not appeal to America's made-with-a-mix mentality. But when the book finally came out in 1961, under the title *Mastering the Art of French Cooking*, it proved a bestseller.

Child's career as America's chief explicator of French cooking reached full bloom in 1963, when she debuted in *The French Chef* on public television. Speaking in a high, chirpy voice, the somewhat gawky Child made mistakes on camera with a "kind of muddleheaded nonchalance." But audiences loved that muddleheadedness, and over the next few years Child became an indisputable force in shaping America's culinary mores. When she beat egg whites with a whisk, suddenly there was a nationwide rush for that implement, and if she used fresh broccoli, supermarket demand for it would soar.

When Hans Namuth photographed Child shopping in an Italian market in Boston's North End in 1977, she was about to begin work on a new television series, titled *Julia Child & Company*. In the previous several years, she had burst "out of the French straitjacket," and among the featured dishes in the new series would be variations on traditional American recipes.

---

# Julia Child
1912–2004
*Chef, author*

HANS NAMUTH
(1915–1990)
Gelatin silver print
24 × 34.8 cm (9⁷⁄₁₆ × 13¹¹⁄₁₆ in.)
1977
Gift of the estate of Hans Namuth

In December 1968, a recent Howard University music graduate named Jessye Norman appeared at Constitution Hall in Washington, D.C., singing the soprano solos in a presentation of Handel's *Messiah*. Among those bowled over by her voice was *Washington Post* critic Paul Hume, who summed up her performance as a "prelude to something quite extraordinary." Twelve months later, that prediction began reaching fulfillment, when Norman's rich, sumptuously smooth voice created a sensation at Berlin's Deutsche Oper in Wagner's *Tannhäuser*.

Over the next several years, Norman was offered many choice roles, but not wanting to fall into the repertoire of the typical soprano diva, she accepted them on a very selective basis. Choosiness, however, did not hamper her artistic growth. Of her interpretation of the Liebestod from *Tristan und Isolde* at a concert in 1974, a reviewer said that she had given "as nearly flawless a performance as one could rightly expect from the human voice."

Between 1975 and 1980, Norman limited her appearances to lieder recitals and orchestra concerts. When she finally returned to opera, she seemed better than ever, and in 1982, her long-delayed American opera debut with the Opera Company of Philadelphia was hailed as "A Modern Norman Conquest."

This image appeared in *Vanity Fair* in 1983. The occasion was the opening of the New York Metropolitan Opera's centenary season, which began with a production of Hector Berlioz's *Les Troyens*, in which Norman took the role of Cassandra. Although this was her first appearance at the Met, she was no stranger to performing with great opera companies, and she had sung Cassandra before. Even so, appearing with her own country's most revered company proved more unnerving than expected. Despite having plenty of time to work out jitters in rehearsal, of her opening-night entrance, she said, "I still turned to jelly."

# Jessye Norman
born 1945
*Singer*

IRVING PENN
(born 1917)
Platinum-palladium print
49 × 47.9 cm (19⁹⁄₁₆ × 18⅞ in.)
1983 (printed 1985)
Gift of Irving Penn

As an undergraduate at Hunter College, Rosalyn Yalow took an afternoon physics course that suffered from post-prandial lethargy. To raise the energy level one day, the professor challenged his students to spot two errors in his presentation. Recalling the incident years later, the professor said that Yalow met the challenge admirably—finding not two mistakes, but three.

Clearly, Yalow was a student with promise, but when she went on to graduate work in physics at the University of Illinois, her gender was sometimes a deterrent to full collegial acceptance. Still, she persevered, and in 1945, she became the second woman at Illinois to complete a doctorate in physics.

After leaving Illinois, Yalow returned to her native New York City to teach at Hunter, and in 1947, she joined the staff of the Bronx Veterans Administration Hospital as a medical physicist charged with exploring the potential of radioisotopes in diagnosing and treating illnesses. Her research entered its most productive phase three years later, when she teamed up with Dr. Solomon Berson. While "he provided the biological brilliance," one colleague recalled, she supplied "the mathematical muscle," and together they made pathbreaking explorations into the use of radioisotopes for a variety of purposes. Out of their investigations came radioimmunoassay—commonly referred to as RIA—a procedure that has had immense value in the diagnosis and treatment of a wide range of diseases. For her part in this collaboration, Yalow became the first woman to win the prestigious Albert Lasker Award for Basic Medical Research, and in 1977, she became the second woman to receive the Nobel Prize in medicine.

This picture was part of a series of images depicting Jewish women from around the world, taken by photographer Arthur Leipzig for his book *Sarah's Daughters*.

Rosalyn Yalow
born 1921
*Medical physicist*

ARTHUR LEIPZIG
(born 1918)
Gelatin silver print
22.1 × 33 cm (8$^{11}/_{16}$ × 13 in.)
1987

When Maya Lin handed in her proposal for a Vietnam War memorial as an exercise in an architecture course at Yale, her professor thought that her design for a low stretch of black marble inscribed with the names of the more than 57,000 soldiers who had died in Vietnam rated no more than a B. It was a respectable grade, but hardly a ringing endorsement. Lin, however, thought well enough of her proposal to submit it to the nationwide design competition for the Vietnam Memorial in Washington, D.C. The contest judges were considerably more impressed with Lin's work than her professor, so much so that they awarded her the commission for the memorial.

Not everyone agreed with the judges' decision, however. One Vietnam veteran denounced Lin's design as "a black gash of shame," and many thought it was a scheme perpetrated by antiwar critics to demean those who had died in Vietnam. But in the end, Lin's original faith in her conception was vindicated. As people streamed past the monument's dark, polished panels upon its completion in 1982 and stopped to touch the incised names of soldiers they had known, it was clear that Lin had struck a chord that in no way dishonored the dead of the Vietnam War. Of all the war memorials across America, there was none that carried deeper meaning for its citizenry.

By the time this photograph was taken in 1988, Lin had established herself as a designer, architect, and sculptor in New York City. She was "tense and uncomfortable" about posing for the picture, photographer Michael Katakis recalled. But then her cat reached out a paw to demand her attention. With that, Lin's "face and hands took on a gentle and vulnerable posture," and Katakis got the kind of image that he had been hoping for.

# Maya Lin
born 1959
*Designer, architect*

MICHAEL KATAKIS
(born 1952)
Gelatin silver print
22.2 × 33.3 cm (8 ¾ × 13 ⅛ in.), 1988
Gift of Michael Katakis in memory of his
father, George E. Katakis

In March 1992, *Time* magazine featured on its cover this image of Susan Faludi standing behind a seated Gloria Steinem. It was a natural and eminently newsworthy pairing. To begin with, both were feminists. While Steinem, founder of *Ms.* magazine, belonged to an older generation of women's movement activists, Faludi, a Pulitzer Prize–winning reporter for the *Wall Street Journal*, represented feminism's younger contingent. They had both also recently published bestselling books that offered two sides of the most recently minted feminist coin.

Faludi's book, *Backlash: The Undeclared War against American Women*, claimed that the progress of women resulting from feminist agitation of the sixties and seventies had eroded in the 1980s as a result of a haphazard coalition of societal forces. Among the chief factors contributing to the erosion, she said, were the myths that feminism was unnecessary because its goals had essentially been achieved, and that many women were now at odds with themselves over the conflicts of child-rearing and career. Faludi proved remarkably deft at challenging such myths, and her book was coming to be regarded as "feminism's new manifesto." After reading her "hair-raising … [but] documented analysis," wrote a critic, "you may never read a magazine or see a movie or walk through a department store the same way again."

Steinem's book, *Revolution from Within: A Book of Self-Esteem*, was more individually oriented, and its central thrust was a contention that the potential for enlarging life's possibilities hinged largely on self-understanding. Some feminists took Steinem to task for writing this book, accusing her of "'abandoning the cause' by subsuming feminism in a model for self-recovery." But Steinem had at least one rejoinder to such charges. "When one member of a group changes," she observed in *Revolution*, "the balance shifts for everyone."

---

# Susan Faludi born 1959
# Gloria Steinem born 1934
*Feminists, writers*

GREGORY HEISLER
(born 1954)
Chromogenic print
31.7 × 25.2 cm (12½ × 9¹⁵/₁₆ in.)
1992
Gift of *Time* magazine

# Notes on Sources

## Preface

Page 9, Amelia Earhart: "You betja!" in Susan Butler, *East to the Dawn: The Life of Amelia Earhart* (Reading, Mass.: Addison-Wesley, 1997), 395. Page 10, Maya Lin: "A memorial of our own times," in *New York Times*, June 29, 1981.

## Gertrude Simmons Bonnin (Zitkala-Ša)

"I was shorn of my branches," in Zitkala-Ša, *American Indian Stories*, with a foreword by Dexter Fisher (Lincoln: University of Nebraska Press, 1985), 97. "Sometimes I think," in David Johnson and Raymond Wilson, "Gertrude Simmons Bonnin, 1876–1938: 'Americanize the First American,'" *American Indian Quarterly* 12 (winter 1988): 38.

## Helen Keller

"Our worst foes," in Helen Keller, *The Story of My Life* (New York: Doubleday, Page & Company, 1904), 434. "Paradise," in Helen Keller, "A Chat about the Hand," *Century* 69 (January 1905): 455.

## Isadora Duncan

"More like a spirit," in *Philadelphia Telegraph*, December 22, 1908. "When she danced," in Arnold Genthe, *As I Remember* (New York: Reynal & Hitchcock, 1936), 198.

## Jeannette Rankin

"The Girl of the Golden West," in Hope Chamberlin, *A Minority of Members* (New York: Praeger, 1973), 7–8. "Now that we have a pull in Congress," in Kevin S. Giles, *Flight of the Dove: The Story of Jeannette Rankin* (Beaverton, Oreg.: Touchstone Press, 1980), 83.

## Margaret Sanger

"Bruised and exhausted," in *New York Times*, March 7, 1917, 20.

## Louise Bryant

"A kingdom more bright," in Barbara Gelb, *So Short a Time: A Biography of John Reed and Louise Bryant* (New York: W.W. Norton, 1973), 167. "The eyes of the people themselves," in Virginia Gardner, *"Friend and Lover": The Life of Louise Bryant* (New York: Horizon Press, 1982), 112.

## Katherine Stinson

"Flying Schoolgirl" and "dippy twist loop," in Lisa Yount, *Women Aviators* (New York: Facts on File, 1995), 4, 6. "The women were wild with excitement," in Valerie Moolman, *Women Aloft* (Alexandria, Va.: Time-Life Books, 1981), 35. "If your airplane," in Yount, *Women Aviators*, 3.

## Mary Pickford

"You're too little and too fat," in Scott Eyman, *Mary Pickford: America's Sweetheart* (New York: Donald I. Fine, 1990), 37. "Appears [in a movie] makes," in Raymond Lee, *The Films of Mary Pickford* (New York: Castle Books, 1970), 20. "Helplessly feminine," in *Vogue*, February 1920, 60.

## Aimee Semple McPherson

"Whoopee evangelist" and "Barnum of religion," in Edward T. James, ed., *Notable American Women, 1607–1950* (Cambridge, Mass.: Belknap Press of Harvard University Press, 1971), vol. 2, 479. "Electrifies every person," in Joseph Henry Steele, "Sister Aimée: Bernhardt of the Sawdust Trail," in *Vanity Fair: Selections from America's Most Memorable Magazine*, ed. Cleveland Amory and Frederic Bradlee (New York: Viking Press, 1977), 237. "MAN BARKS," in Daniel Mark Epstein, *Sister Aimee: The Life of Aimee Semple McPherson* (New York: Harcourt Brace Jovanovich, 1993), 212.

## Gertrude Stein with Jo Davidson

"Soporific rigamaroles," in *Time*, September 11, 1933, 59. "Wives are a great recognition," in *Vanity Fair*, February 1923, 48.

## Lillian Gish

"Played so many frail, downtrodden little virgins," in Louise M. Collins and Lorna M. Mabunda, eds., *The Annual Obituary 1993* (London: St. James Press, 1994), 146. "She is not Hawthorne's," in Anna Rothe, ed., *Current Biography, 1944* (New York: H.W. Wilson, 1945), 241.

## Doris Humphrey

"Never stops wondering," in John Garraty and Mark C. Carnes, eds., *American National Biography* (New York: Oxford University Press, 1999), vol. 11, 467. "As the granite," in *New York Times*, January 11, 1959, 12.

## Josephine Baker

"There was something about her rhythm," in Charles Moritz, ed., *Current Biography, 1964*, 20. "A scream of salutation," in *New York Times*, April 13, 1975. "Nefertiti of now" and "beautiful panther," in Lynn Haney, *Naked at the Feast: A Biography of Josephine Baker* (New York: Dodd, Mead, 1981), 67–68.

## Willa Cather

"An erasure of personality," in *Dictionary of American Biography* (New York: Charles Scribner's Sons, 1974), supp. 4, 153. "Set in Nebraska," in Deborah Carlin, "Willa Cather," in *Modern American Women Writers* (New York: Charles Scribner's Sons, 1991), 55. "Touched with genius," "literary artistry," and "an American classic," in James Woodress, *Willa Cather: A Literary Life* (Lincoln: University of Nebraska Press, 1987), 240, 409–10. "A stylist of precision and beauty," in *Vanity Fair*, April 1927, 65. "Heir apparent," in *Vanity Fair*, July 1927, 30.

## Malvina Hoffman

"Might not be a defect" and "as if she had wings," in *New York Times*, July 11, 1966, 29.

## Berenice Abbott

"How about me," "I had no idea," and "most of them were good," in Hank O'Neal, *Berenice Abbott: American Photographer* (New York: McGraw Hill, 1982), 9–10.

## Pearl S. Buck

"The most distinguished work," in Marjorie Dent Candee, ed., *Current Biography, 1956*, 83.

## Eleanor Holm and Helene Madison

"Looks, grace, and carriage" and "a human torpedo boat," in Robert S. McFee, "Ladies from Olympus," *Vanity Fair*, September 1932, 31. "Uncanny ability to manipulate reality," in Mary Panzer, "Steichen," *American Photo* 12 (January/February 2001): 76.

## Katharine Hepburn

"Miss Hepburn … may one day" and "like a woman who has at last found the joy," in Gary Carey, *Katharine Hepburn: A Hollywood Yankee* (New York: St Martin's Press, 1983), 66, 110.

## Emma Goldman

"Red Emma," in *New York Times*, February 2, 1934, 9. "No. I was always considered bad," in *New York Times*, February 3, 1934, 15. "Who the hell wants to be reasonable?" in *Newsweek*, January 20, 1934, 20.

## Mae West

"Come up and see me some time," in *Time*, October 16, 1933, 14. "Between two evils," in *New York Times*, November 23, 1980. "What once looked like hearty bawdiness," in Emily Leider, *Becoming Mae West* (New York: Farrar, Straus & Giroux, 1997), 314.

## Martha Graham

"Ugly girl makes ugly movements," in Susan Ware, *Letter to the World: Seven Women Who Shaped the American Century* (New York: W.W. Norton, 1998), 213. "Letters comparing him," in Don McDonagh, *Martha Graham: A Biography* (New York: Praeger, 1973), 115. "A miracle of intuition," in Agnes De Mille, *Martha: The Life and Work of Martha Graham* (New York: Random House, 1991), 244. "No artist is ahead of his time," in Merle Armitage, ed., *Martha Graham: The Early Years* (New York: Da Capo Press, 1978), 107.

## Helen Hayes
"Re-creates not only," in Donn B. Murphy and Stephen Moore, *Helen Hayes: A Bio-Bibliography* (Westport, Conn.: Greenwood Press, 1993), 109. "Seen anything like the ovation," in *New York Times*, March 18, 1993, B9. "By some alchemy," in *Time*, December 30, 1935, 22.

## Anna May Wong
"Rose blushing through ivory," in *New York Times*, February 4, 1961.

## Elizabeth Hawes
"ALL REDDISH BROWN OR BLACK PRINTS" and "absolutely out of fashion," in Bettina Berch, *Radical by Design: The Life and Style of Elizabeth Hawes* (New York: E.P. Dutton, 1988), 30, 29. "A complete anachronism," in *Newsweek*, March 28, 1938, 29.

## Shirley Temple
"Boom in Child Stars," in *Time*, July 25, 1938, 25. "Shame on them!" in *New York Times*, July 18, 1938, 12.

## Carmel Snow
"Voice of American fashion," in *New York Times*, May 9, 1961, 39. "You can't keep an exciting fashion down," in Jane Trahey, *Harper's Bazaar* (New York: Random House, 1967), 90.

## Katharine Cornell
"Got worse as the years went on," "I don't think," and "something electric happened," in *New York Times*, June 10, 1974. "Had something in it," in *New York Times*, December 13, 1924, 12. "An actress of the first order," in William C. Young, ed., *Famous Actors and Actresses of the American Stage* (New York: R.R. Bowker Company, 1975), vol. 1, 220–21.

## Margaret Bourke-White
"Life's Margaret Bourke-White Goes Bombing," in *Life*, March 1, 1943, 17. "The most famous on-the-spot," in *Washington Post*, June 29, 1989. "It does no good," in Margaret Bourke-White, *Portrait of Myself* (New York: Simon and Schuster, 1963), 250.

## Dorothy Parker

"Blend of Little Nell," in *New York Times*, June 8, 1967, 38. "That's queer" and "Excuse my dust," in Robert E. Drennan, *The Algonquin Wits* (New York: Citadel Press, 1985), 116, 125. "What's a couple of sandspits," in Marion Meade, *Dorothy Parker: What Fresh Hell Is This?* (New York: Villard Books, 1988), 319.

## Pearl Primus

"If ever a young dancer," in Lynne Fauley Emery, *Black Dance from 1619 to Today* (Princeton, N.J.: Princeton Book Co., 1988), 262. "Her forte is force," in *Time*, August 25, 1947, 42. "Dance is my medicine," in Barbara Carlisle Bigelow, ed., *Contemporary Black Biography* (Detroit: Gale Research, 1994), vol. 6, 214.

## Mary Lou Williams

"One of the very few capable female jazz musicians," in *Life*, October 11, 1943, 120. "If you shut your eyes," in *Time*, July 26, 1943, 76. "The Lady Who Swings the Band," in Linda Dahl, *Stormy Weather: The Music and Lives of a Century of Jazzwomen* (New York: Pantheon Books, 1984), 62. "A spectacle *non pareil*," in Gjon Mili, *Photographs and Recollections of Gjon Mili* (Boston: New York Graphic Society, 1980), 168.

## Hannah Arendt

"The most brilliant," in Irving Kristol, "A Treasure of the Future," *New Republic*, July 10, 1961, 19. "Isn't that marvelous!" in *New York Times*, December 6, 1975, 32.

## Marian Anderson

"A voice like yours," in *Time*, December 30, 1946, 59. "Mistress of all she surveyed," in Allan Keiler, *Marian Anderson: A Singer's Journey* (New York: Scribner, 2000), 161. "Designed for hand to hand combat," *New York Times*, April 9, 1993.

## Peggy Guggenheim

"A member not of the Lost" and "just as well lose," in Aline B. Saarinen, *The Proud Possessors* (New York: Random House, 1958), 327, 331.

## Gypsy Rose Lee

"You don't have to be naked," in *Life*, May 27, 1957, 104. "Seven minutes of sheer art," in *Life*, December 14, 1942, 99. "Queenly style," in *Life*, May 27, 1957, 104.

## Mildred "Babe" Didrikson Zaharias

"*I'm* the star," in Ware, *Letter to the World*, 199. "She must be Superman's sister" and "I just loosen my girdle," in *Time*, June 23, 1947, 66. "Queen of the Links," in *New York Daily News*, October 12, 1947.

## Lillian Hellman

"It was like a Chinese box," and "Put a good-looking man," in William Wright, *Lillian Hellman: The Image, the Woman* (New York: Simon and Schuster, 1986), 149, 36.

## Billie Holiday

"The greatest female jazz voice" and "iridescent gems," in Jessie Carney Smith, ed., *Notable Black American Women* (Detroit: Gale Research, 1992), 500–501. "Every major pop singer," in Deborah G. Felder, *The 100 Most Influential Women of All Time: A Ranking Past and Present* (Secaucus, N.J.: Carol Publishing Group, 1996), 318. "Hysterical applause" and "That's all over now," in *Time*, April 12, 1948, 68–69.

## Georgia O'Keeffe

"I began to realize" and "to fill space in a beautiful way," in Katharine Kuh, *The Artist's Voice* (New York: Harper & Row, 1962), 189, 190. "The unflickering flame of a candle," in Laurie Lisle, *Portrait of an Artist: A Biography of Georgia O'Keeffe* (New York: Seaview Books, 1980), 123.

## Helena Rubinstein

"It doesn't matter how shaky," in *Time*, April 9, 1965, 98. "I tell you I am a worker," and "a John D. Rockefeller in petticoated miniature," in Hambla Bauer, "Beauty Tycoon," *Collier's*, December 4, 1948, 16.

## Margaret Mead

"I expect to die," in Ware, *Letter to the World*, 122. "A friendly but determined-looking woman," and "technical terms," in Harvey Briet, "Talk with Margaret Mead," *New York Times*, October 30, 1949, pt. 7, 41.

## Anna Mary Robertson ("Grandma") Moses

"Most of us would be bored," in *Washington Star*, July 24, 1945. "It's nice to be here," in *New York Times*, May 15, 1949, 58.

## Eleanor Roosevelt

"Reversed the usual lot," "become, perhaps, the best known woman," and "the most popular living American," in *Time*, October 25, 1948, 25. "Could have made no better selection," in *Time*, September 13, 1943, 20. "Naïveté and cunning," in Joseph Lash, *Eleanor: The Years Alone* (New York: W.W. Norton, 1972), 69.

## Ethel Waters, Carson McCullers, and Julie Harris

"Masterly," "wonderfully, almost painfully, perceptive," and "rich and eloquent," in *New York Times*, January 6, 1950, 26. "A new star in the theater," in *Life*, January 23, 1950, 63.

## Frances Perkins

"The last leaf on the tree," in Lillian Holmen Mohr, *Frances Perkins: That Woman in FDR's Cabinet!* (Croton-on-Hudson, N.Y.: North River Press, 1979), 288. "Woozy in the head," "grim, polite, and unimpressed," and "The accusation that I am a woman," in *Time*, May 21, 1965, 31. "The argument can be made," in *Time*, December 25, 1944, 14.

## Carmelita Maracci

"Here is a remarkable," "seated throughout," and "an abstract of Spain in the dance," in *New York Times*, June 27, 1937, 8.

## Marianne Moore

"I never knew anyone," in Jane Howard, "Leading Lady of U.S. Verse," *Life*, January 13, 1967, 40. "Among the noblest lyrics," in *New York Times*, February 6, 1972, 40. "Just about the most accomplished poetess alive," in *Time*, December 10, 1951, 112. "It ought to be work to read," in *New York Times*, February 6, 1972, 40. "As for Gil Hodges," in Marianne Moore, *The Complete Poems of Marianne Moore* (New York: Macmillan, 1967), 183. "These knowers," in *Life*, September 21, 1953, 205.

## Ella Fitzgerald

"Renovate," "came to inhabit," and "I never knew how good," in *Washington Post*, June 17, 1996, pt. C, 2. "In a frenzy" and "the roar was deafening," in Stuart Nicholson, *Ella Fitzgerald: A Biography of the First Lady of Jazz* (New York: Charles Scribner's Sons, 1993), 148.

## Judy Garland

"The star of her own adult melodrama," in *New York Times*, June 29, 1969. "Unhinged," in Gerald Clarke, *Get Happy: The Life of Judy Garland* (New York: Random House, 2000), 318. "Just about the greatest," in *Time*, October 25, 1954, 86. "Knowing that he had heard," in *Time*, May 5, 1961, 52.

## Marilyn Monroe

"The best thing that ever happened to me" and "I never felt like a star," in *Marilyn Monroe and the Camera* (Boston: Little, Brown and Company, 1989), 116, 239. "Three luminous minutes" and "week's torment," in *New York Times*, August 6, 1962, 13.

## Dorothy Day

"The nearest," in *Time*, December 15, 1980, 74. "When they say you are a saint," in Moritz, *Current Biography, 1962*, 96. "Quiet, even shy," in Vivian Cherry and Sarah S. Appleton, "The Catholic Worker," *Jubilee* 3 (July 1955): 32.

## Althea Gibson

"Althea Gibson is not the most graceful," and "she plays smarter all the time," in *Time*, August 26, 1957, 44, 47.

## Sylvia Plath

"I have … overcome," in Sylvia Plath, *The Journals of Sylvia Plath* (New York: Dial Press, 1982), 307.

## Anne Sexton

"Read splendidly," "Once the parties started," and "I was scared the whole time," in Diane Wood Middlebrook, *Anne Sexton: A Biography* (New York: Vintage Books, 1992), 140, 138.

## Joan Baez

"As lustrous and rich," in *New York Times*, November 13, 1961, 42. "One of the medals which hangs over my heart," in Joan Baez, *And a Voice to Sing With: A Memoir* (New York: Summit Books, 1987), 103.

## Diana Ross, with fellow Supremes Florence Ballard and Mary Wilson

"Swerves into the most unsupple lyrics" and "slung like six feet of limp wrist," in *New York Times*, July 23, 1967, pt. 2, 11. "I enjoyed them as people," in Bruce Davidson, *Portraits* (New York: Aperture, 1999), 5.

## Fannie Lou Hamer

"We didn't come all this way" and "I'm sick and tired of being sick and tired," in Smith, *Notable Black American Women*, 443–44.

## Janis Joplin

"Just 'silly crazy Janis,'" in Michael Lydon, "The Janis Joplin Philosophy: Every Moment She Is What She Feels," *The New York Times Biographical Edition*, 1969 (New York: New York Times, 1969), 1384. "When I can't sing," in *Newsweek*, February 24, 1969, 84.

## Pauline Trigère

"You see?" in Amy Fine Collins, "Every Inch an Original," *Vanity Fair*, December 1999, 347. "Virtuoso with the shears," in Jack Alexander, "New York's Queen of Fashion," *Saturday Evening Post*, April 18, 1961, 90. "Put a piece of fabric," in Moritz, *Current Biography, 1960*, 435.

## Diane Arbus

"Giving a camera" and "truly generous spirit," in Doon Arbus and Marvin Israel, eds., *Diane Arbus: Magazine Work* (New York: Aperture, 1984), 161, 165.

## Diana Vreeland

"Why don't you ... sweep," in Ted Burke, "Mrs. Vreeland," *Town & Country* 129 (June 1975): 82. "Tremble[d] at her nod" and "to pick purely," in *Time*, May 10, 1963, 53. "A bird of paradise" and "melted into the background," in Burke, "Mrs. Vreeland," 79.

## Katharine Graham

"I ... shut my eyes," in *Washington Post*, July 18, 2001. "Most powerful woman in journalism," in *Time*, February 7, 1977, 70. "The guts of a burglar," in *Washington Post*, July 18, 2001.

## Barbara Jordan

"A bit like grilling God" and "never wanted to be run of the mill," in *New York Times*, January 18, 1996. "The best mind on the committee," in Moritz, *Current Biography, 1974*, 190. "Overstate the solemnness," in Mary Beth Rogers, *Barbara Jordan: American Hero* (New York: Bantam Books, 1998), 214.

## Julia Child

"Cordon Bleu widower," in Noël Riley Fitch, *Appetite for Life: The Biography of Julia Child* (New York: Doubleday, 1997), 175. "Kind of muddleheaded nonchalance," in *Time*, March 20, 1964, 56. "Out of the French straitjacket," in Fitch, *Appetite for Life*, 398.

## Jessye Norman

"Prelude to something quite extraordinary," in *Washington Post*, December 30, 1968.
"As nearly flawless a performance," in Moritz, *Current Biography, 1976*, 295. "A Modern
Norman Conquest," in *Newsweek*, December 6, 1982, 128. "I still turned to jelly," in
*New York Times*, September 27, 1983.

## Rosalyn Yalow

"He provided the biological brilliance," in Elizabeth Stone, "Madame Curie from the
Bronx," *New York Times Magazine*, April 9, 1970, 95.

## Maya Lin

"A black gash of shame," in *Time*, November 9, 1981, 103. "Tense and uncomfortable" and
"face and hands," in Michael Katakis to Ann Shumard, November 23, 1991, curatorial files,
National Portrait Gallery.

## Susan Faludi and Gloria Steinem

"Feminism's new manifesto," in Judith Graham, ed., *Current Biography, 1993*, 187. "Hair-
raising," in Laura Shapiro, "Why Women Are Angry," *Newsweek*, October 21, 1991, 41.
"'Abandoning the cause'" and "When one member of a group changes," in *Time*, March 9,
1992, 41.

# Index

Page numbers in *italics* refer to illustrations.
Page numbers in **bold** refer to main entries.

# Photography Credits

*The publishers have made every effort to trace and contact copyright holders of the photographs reproduced in this book; they will be happy to correct in subsequent editions any errors or omissions that are brought to their attention.*